QUO VADIS, PETRE?

(Where are you going, Peter?)

**A filial request for orientation to the Vicar of Christ
from many Catholic faithful
in face of the panreligious festivities
planned for the celebration of the
passing of the Millennium**

QUO VADIS, PETRE?

**A filial request for orientation
to the Vicar of Christ
from many Catholic faithful
in face of the panreligious festivities
planned for the celebration of the passing
of the Milennium**

A Special Edition to the 11-volume Collection
Eli, Eli, lamma sabacthani?

Atila Sinke Guimarães

Translated and edited by
Marian Therese Horvat, Ph.D.

ISBN 0-967-2166-5

Library of Congress Catalog Card Number: 99-62971

Printed and bound in the United States of America.

Tradition **I**n **A**ction, Inc.
P.O. Box 23135
Los Angeles, CA 90023

The Appian Way was the most important of the consular roads that radiated from Rome to the distant provinces of the Empire. The church *Domine, quo vadis?* was erected on the spot where Jesus was said to appear to St. Peter, who, concerned about the fierce persecution of the Emperor Nero, was leaving Rome.

Peter asked Him, *"Domine, quo vadis?"* (Lord, where are You going?) And Christ responded, "I am going to Rome to be crucified a second time." The Apostle, understanding the censure, went back into the City, where he was imprisoned and martyred.

NOTICE TO THE READER

The book *Quo vadis, Petre?* (Where are you going, Peter?) is a special edition to the 11-volume Collection *Eli, Eli, lamma sabacthani?* ("My God, My God, Why Hast Thou Foresaken Me?") The first volume – *In the Murky Waters of Vatican II* – was published in 1997. The next volume is presently in the process of translation and publication. The collection analyzes the letter, spirit, and fruits of the Council.

Ecumenism and inter-religious dialogue are examined in Volume V, which studies in detail the so-called "theological pluralism" that presents the notion of the "Church of Christ" as being different from the Catholic Church. It examines the theory of the "anonymous Christian," which states that normally there would be salvation outside the ambit of Holy Mother Church. This volume also carefully analyzes the consequences of ecumenism and inter-religious dialogue, which tend toward bringing together the diverse confessions into a single whole. The final goal would be the establishment of a panreligion. This book *Quo vadis, Petre?* is an analysis of ecumenism and inter-religious dialogue in relation to the festivities planned for the passing of the Millennium.

Quo vadis, Petre? is a work that stands by itself and completes the vision presented in Volume V. For this reason it is considered a special issue of The Collection *Eli, Eli, lamma sabacthani?*

* * *

TABLE OF CONTENTS

CODE OF CANON LAW

"Can. 212 – § 2. The Christian faithful are free to make known their needs, especially spiritual ones, and their desires to the pastors of the Church.

"§ 3. In accord with the knowledge, competence and preeminence which they possess, they [the faithful] have the right and even at times a duty to manifest to the sacred Pastors their opinion on matters which pertain to the good of the Church, and they have a right to make their opinion known to the other Christian faithful, with due regard for the integrity of Faith and Morals and reverence toward their Pastors, and with consideration for the common good and the dignity of persons."[1]

---

[1] *The Code of Canon Law* promulgated by John Paul II, Washington D.C.: The Canon Law Society of America, 1983, p. 71.

Los Angeles, April 3, 1999

His Holiness John Paul II
Apostolic Palace
Vatican City

Most Holy Father,

In choosing the title of the work, the author deliberately selected one that echoes that timeless and respected tradition regarding St. Peter, who was leaving Rome along the *Via Appia* because of the mounting persecutions of Christians in the Eternal City. At a certain moment on his journey out of Rome, Our Lord appeared to the Vicar of Christ on earth, who asked Him: *"Domine, quo vadis?"* (Lord, where are you going?) And the Lord answered him, "I am going to Rome to be crucified a second time." Undoubtedly, it was an admonition from the Redeemer to the Prince of the Apostles. His mission was to be fulfilled in Rome, notwithstanding defeats, imprisonment, and his future martyrdom. This is a beautiful narration that stimulates courage and that has remained in the memory and sense of the faithful through the centuries! A tradition whose authenticity and venerability are attested to, among innumerable other proofs, by the Church that was built at the Roman site where the event took place.

These words were chosen in order to emphasize the desire of so many Roman Catholics for doctrinal direction. The author's attitude is one of filial love for, and highest dedication to, the sacred institution of the Papacy and of enthusiastic acceptance of the superiority of the Sovereign Pontiff over every other earthly potentate – especially over the simple faithful – as described in the sublime words of St. Gregory VII in *Dictatus Papae* and H. H. Boniface VIII in *Unam Sanctam*. May this letter be considered only as a humble request for enlightenment to relieve the increasing bewilderment of innumerable Catholics. It is, therefore, with a heart filled with respect and with a spirit numbed with perplexity that we[2] direct ourselves to the "sweet Christ on Earth," quoting that expression of St. Catherine of Siena.[3]

*

We have heard from the lips of innumerable pastors that the faithful, and especially the laity, have an important role to play in the Church and that this implies both rights and duties. Therefore, Most Holy Father, permit us, who rely upon these rights – so often repeated since the Ecumenical Council Vatican II – and seek to fulfil our duty, to raise our voices even to the See of the Vicar of Christ. We hope that Your Holiness, accessible to the requests of so many who find themselves outside the bosom of the Holy Catholic Church, will receive with pleasure and kind attention this manifestation of the concerns of her legitimate sons.

The objective of this study is twofold: an analysis of the eventual results of the panreligious festivities that are being pre-

---

[2] The author of this document has spoken with many Catholics about the topic addressed here. A large number of them agreed with the content of the work and shared the concerns of the author. For this reason, although he has no official delegation, the author employs the first person plural "we" in directing statements to the Holy Father and not the first person singular "I."

[3] Johannes Joergensen, *Santa Catarina de Sena*, Petropolis: Vozes, 1953, p. 185.

pared for the passing of the Millennium; and an analysis of some of the consequences of ecumenism and inter-religious dialogue, which will be considered in relation to these festivities.

* * *

CHAPTER I

STATUS QUAESTIONIS

HOW PREPARATIONS FOR THE
MILLENNIUM ARE BEING PRESENTED BY
VATICAN ORGANS AND PRESS

The *status quaestionis* of the preparations for the Millennium can be presented as follows:

1. A Panreligious Meeting in Rome

At the official presentation of the calendar of ceremonies for the passing of the Millennium, Cardinal Roger Etchegaray, president of the Central Committee for the Great Jubilee, announced that a panreligious meeting would take place in Rome in the month of October 1999. This meeting would appear to be a grand scale repetition of the interconfessional journey in Assisi (1986).[4] At a press conference, the Cardinal stated: "Shortly

---

[4] The panreligious journey in Assisi on October 27, 1986 took place in the presence of Your Holiness and representatives of innumerable other confessions, including members of African and American Indian tribes. Apart from the authenticity of these representatives, which was contested by some, the meeting raised controversy because of its ecumenical aspects. To cite only one example, during a prayer session Buddhist monks placed the statue of Buddha over the Tabernacle of the altar. Cardinal Silvio Oddi made this report: "On that day .... I walked through Assisi .... and I saw real profanations in some of the places of

after the opening of the Jubilee, an inter-religious meeting will be held in Rome – with a pilgrimage to Assisi, probably from October 24 to 28 of 1999."[5] Prior to this, press spokesman of the Holy See, Dr. Joaquim Navarro-Vals, made a similar announcement: "In *Tertio millennio adveniente*, the Holy Father points to 1999 as a year that will include a meeting with the other religions, along with other activities. Therefore, among the various initiatives to celebrate the year 2000, the Council of the Presidency of the Great Jubilee has asked the Pontifical Council for Inter-religious Dialogue to organize an Inter-religious Assembly. Having obtained approval for this project, we can now announce that in the second half of October 1999 there will be an

---

prayer. I saw Buddhists dancing around the altar, upon which they placed Buddha in the place of Christ and then incensed it and showed it reverence. A Benedictine protested and the police took him away. ... There was obvious confusion in the faces of the Catholics who were assisting at the ceremony." ("Confissões de um Cardeal," Interview granted to Tommaso Ricci, in *30 Dias*, November 1990, p. 64).

The Old Testament relates how one of the kings, Manasses, commited the crime of placing an idol in the Temple of the Lord (4 Kg. 21:7; 2 Par. 33:7). God punished this action with the destruction of Jerusalem by the Assyrians (4 Kg. 21:10-15; Dan. 12:11). Various Scripture commentators have held that this sacrilege of Manasses gave origin to the expression "the abomination of the desolation installed itself in the Holy Place," a phrase employed in Holy Scripture.

How can one not compare this event from the Old Testament with the enthronement of a statue of Buddha over the Tabernacle of a Catholic Church in Assisi?

Since 1986 interconfessional meetings have been celebrated every year on the same date in different cities. The most significant were those of 1988 in Rome, of 1993 again in Assisi, and of 1994 in the Vatican itself. Habitually they have counted upon the presence of Your Holiness.

[5] Roger Etchegaray, "Conferenza stampa - Gli interventi di presentazione del Calendario dell'Anno Santo 2000," in *L'Osservatore Romano*, 5/27/98, p. 5.

inter-religious assembly in Rome whose theme will be *On the Threshold of the Third Millennium: Collaboration with the Different Religions.* "The encounter will unfold with various events over a period of time. There will be plenary assemblies, work sessions, a journey of pilgrimage – probably to Assisi, a final prayer journey that will include a fast and prayer in various places for each religious community, and a closing ceremony in St. Peter's Square in the presence of the Holy Father."[6]

In your April 1994 document, *Reflections about the Great Jubilee of the Year 2000,* You already alluded to this possibility. In fact, You stated there: "Perhaps the year 2000 could be the occasion for the celebration of something like a pan-Christian meeting. It is a question that should be reflected upon and prayed about, and eventually discussed with the World Council of Churches and with the Council of Orthodox Churches that is now forming."[7]

Everything points to the fact that we are facing the preparation of an Assisi of even greater scope. With this new encounter, the veritable earthquake occasioned by the journey of 1986, which caused tremors in the Church from one end to the other, would be repeated in more significant proportions.

Unfortunately, this is not all. The present secretary general of the World Council of Churches, Protestant pastor Konrad Raiser, proposed for the year 2000 an ecumenical council involving all of the so-called Christian religions – Catholic, Orthodox, and Protestant. Raiser called for the convening of a "truly ecumenical" council that would bring together "all the great families of Christian churches .... so that they may discuss

---

[6] Joaquin Navarro-Vals, "Dichiarazioni del Direttore della Sala Stampa," in *Vatican Information Service,* 3/2/98, Internet Site.

[7] John Paul II, "Riflessioni sul Grande Giubileo dell'anno Duemila," apud L. Accattoli, "Chiesa santa e peccatrice," in *Corriere della Sera,* 4/16/94.

in a collegial atmosphere some of the still unresolved and insurmountable problems of our days – among them the Papacy – in order to give a strong and clear stimulus to the full reconciliation of all the disciples of Jesus."[8]

This proposal was made on the eve of your trip to Germany (June 21-23, 1996). There was no report of any response, even an indirect one. The following month, however, Msgr. Eleuterio F. Fortino, under-secretary of the Pontifical Council for the Promotion of Christian Unity, told the French newspaper *La Croix*: "The Pontifical Council for the Promotion of Christian Unity has given its nod of approval to Konrad Raiser's suggestion to hold a 'universal Christian council' around the year 2000." It is a "proposal fully shared by the Vatican," said Msgr. Fortino.[9]

Another source provided further details. Italian news bulletin *Adista* added that Msgr. Fortino, who is also vice-president of the Ecumenical Commission for the Great Jubilee, accepted Raiser's proposal for a council in the year 2000 "in its general lines." He said that this would be a type of "affirmation of the Apostolic Letter *Tertio millennio adveniente*."[10]

In a document sent to ENI (Ecumenical News International), Msgr. Fortino wrote: "In its general lines, Dr. Raiser's statement appears to us to be an affirmation of the Apostolic Letter *Tertio millennio adveniente*. It says that 'the approaching end of the second millennium calls on everyone to make an examination of conscience and timely ecumenical initiatives so that even if we are not united at the time of the Great Jubilee, we may at least be closer to overcoming divisions in the second millennium (no. 34)' ....

---

[8] *Confronti*, "Verso un concilio ignorato dal Papa," July-August 1996, in *Adista*, 7/6/96, pp. 11f.

[9] "Ecumenisme," in *La Croix*, 7/30/96.

[10] "Sul Concilio universale frenava anche Mons. Fortino. Precisazione," in *Adista*, 10/26/96, pp. 2f.

"For the celebration of the year 2000, when all Christians recall the advent of Christ in History, Pope John Paul II desires 'a meaningful pan-Christian meeting' ... As I read this statement of the general secretariat of the World Council of Churches, I had the impression of a conversation between fellow travelers on the same pilgrimage, supported on the staff of common faith."[11]

Days after this proposal of the Protestant general secretariat, Archbishop John Quinn of San Francisco made a similar proposition at the University of Oxford (6/29/96): "I believe it would greatly benefit both the unity and the effectiveness of the Church if a council were held to mark the beginning of the new millennium."[12]

Based on the statements of Msgrs. Fortino and Quinn, the serious possibility exists that the panreligious meeting planned for October could last for two months and cross the threshold of the year 2000. It could become one of the most expressive of the assemblies of the various religions. Thus, the hypothesis of a pan-Christian meeting being transformed into a council gains in probability.

---

[11] Ibid.

[12] Msgr. John Quinn, "The Exercise of the Primacy - Facing the Cost of Christian Unity," in *Commonweal,* July 12, 96, p. 17.

2. A Common Martyrology

In the Encyclical *Ut unum sint,* You speak about establishing a common martyrology.[13] According to this, it would be desirable for Catholics, Orthodox, and Protestants to share common "saints." Your Holiness affirms the following:

"I have mentioned the will of the Father and the spiritual space in which each community hears the call to overcome the obstacles to unity. All Christian Communities know that, thanks to the power given by the Spirit, obeying that will and overcoming those obstacles are not beyond their reach. All of them in fact have martyrs for the Christian faith. Despite the tragedy of our divisions, these brothers and sisters have preserved an attachment to Christ and to the Father so radical and absolute as to lead even to the shedding of blood. But is not this same attachment at the heart of what I have called a 'dialogue of conversion'? Is it not precisely this dialogue which clearly shows the need for an ever more profound experience of the truth if full communion is to be attained?

"In a theocentric vision, we Christians already have a common *martyrology.* This also includes the martyrs of our own century, more numerous than one might think, and it shows how, at a profound level, God preserves communion among the baptized in the supreme demand of faith, manifested in the sacrifice of life itself. The fact that one can die for the faith shows that other demands of the faith can also be met. I have already remarked, and with deep joy, how an imperfect but real communion is preserved and is growing at many levels of ecclesial life. I now add that this communion is already perfect in what

---

[13] The Catholic Martyrology includes not only those who died as martyrs, as the name suggests, but also other saints who have died without shedding blood in testimony of the Faith. This ecumenical martyrology would use a similar criteria for "martyrs" and "saints" of the various religions. Here we will deal first with the "martyrs" common to diverse religions, and then with the "saints."

we all consider the highest point of the life of grace, *martyria*
unto death, the truest communion possible with Christ who shed
his blood, and by that sacrifice brings near those who once were
far off (cf. Eph. 2:13)."[14]

Therefore, Your Holiness sets forth without hesitation
that there can normally be salvation outside the bosom of the
Holy Catholic Church. Further, You defend the thesis that those
who die giving their blood in defense of their own religions are
all true martyrs.

At this point, You touch upon the question of those who
die by shedding their blood, the so-called "martyrs" of the other
religions. Various press reports have given estimates about the
number of persons who would be considered "martyrs" according to this new criterion.

One reliable Italian newspaper comments: "According to
studies, there would be an average of 300,000 persons [sic] per
year killed for the faith in the '90s. These are the ones who the
Pope in the Sunday *Angelus* qualified as 'true martyrs of the
twentieth century': the Catholics and the Orthodox who in the
Eastern European countries or in other parts of the world were
persecuted 'by an implacable atheist power.' The Pontiff has
already spoken of this in *Tertio millennio adveniente*[15] and in all

---

[14] John Paul II, Encyclical *Ut unum sint*, of May 25, 1995 in *The
Encyclicals of John Paul II*, Ed. J. Michael Milter, CSB, Huntington, IN:
Our Sunday Visitor Publishing Division, 1996, nos. 83f.

[15] * "At the end of the second millennium, the Church has once again
become a Church of martyrs. The persecution of believers – priests,
religious, and laity – has caused a great sowing of martyrdom in different parts of the world. The witness to4 Christ borne even to the shedding of the blood has become a common inheritance of Catholics,
Orthodox, Anglicans, and Protestants .... In our own century the martyrs have returned, many of them nameless, *unknown soldiers* as it
were of God's great cause" (Apostolic Letter *Tertio millennio
adveniente*, of November 10, 1994, no. 37).
* "Is not the twentieth century a time of great witness, which extends
even to the shedding of blood? And does not this witness also involve

the ecumenical documents of the last years. What is the number of the martyrs of communism, victims of the 'red way'? Last year John Paul II appointed a 'commission for the new martyrs' as a preparatory committee for Jubilee 2000. The criteria for compiling a list of those who died for the faith in this century will be chosen by representatives of the churches of the whole world. There would be 200,000 ministers of worship assassinated in the ex-USSR alone."[16]

Archbishop Crescenzio Sepe, secretary general of the Great Jubilee Committee for the Year 2000, has also released statements about the meaning of the "new martyrs" who will be declared on the occasion of the Millennium: "One will no longer speak only of the Catholic martyrs of the 20th century. We will make an ecumenical ceremony to commemorate the Orthodox and so many others – Christian or not – who gave their lives for others, above all in the decades of the terrors of Communism, Nazism, and other dictatorships. On a day specifically dedicated to the modern martyrs, various names and special cases will be remembered."[17]

The statement of Msgr. Sepe that "we will make an ecumenical ceremony to commemorate the Orthodox and so many others – Christian or not – who gave their lives for others" clearly indicates that there will be Jewish and Muslim "martyrs"

---

the various Churches and Ecclesial Communities which take their name from Christ, crucified and risen? (*Ut unum sint*, no. 48, Robert Moynihan and Antonio Gaspari, "Can Changing The Papacy Bring Unity?" in *Inside the Vatican*, June-July, 1995).

* "In a theocentric vision, we Christians already have a common martyrology. This also includes martyrs of our own century, more numerous than one might think" (Ibid., no. 84).

[16] "I nuovi martiri? Le vittime di un ateismo totalitario," in *Corriere della Sera*, 8/28/96.

[17] Crescenzio Sepe, Press statement, apud Federico Mandillo, "A igreja faz preparativos para o Grande Jubileu," in *Estado de S. Paulo*, 11/2/98.

as well. This calls to mind the words of Your Holiness upon receiving Yitszak Rabin's widow Leah when You told her that he "died a martyr of peace."[18]

Thus, the perspective of a common martyrology that, strictly speaking, should include Jews, would probably contain victims of the concentration camps as well as Muslims. In the latter case, would Catholics have to venerate as "martyrs" the innumerable Mohammedans killed during the Crusades? Would it be possible for the two antagonist religions, for which the followers of each side died in armed combat, to be equally true to the point that their members would receive analogous homage? One could say that this would be the negation of the principle of contradiction.

Another serious concern is that the year 2000 could see the possible beatification of heretics who were condemned to death for their doctrines. For example, Girolamo Savonarola, Giordano Bruno, and Jan Hus could also come to be considered "martyrs."[19]

---

[18] John Paul II, Statements, in *Jornal do Brasil*, 12/15/95.

[19] **Girolamo Savonarola** (1452-1498), a Dominican monk who under the pretext of combating the moral excesses of the Renaissance and the Clergy, preached a "miserabilist" Church, without earthly goods (see Note 46). With the help of King Charles VIII of France, he established a theocratic republic of a socialist bent in Florence. He disobeyed the orders of his ecclesiastical superiors and was excommunicated. He continued to preach, calling for a council against the Pope. The people apprehended him, he was handed over to justice, and was burned at the stake. He is considered the precursor of the Reforma-tion, and his statue stands in front of a monument dedicated to Luther in Worms.

Giordano Bruno (1548-1600), a Dominican monk, was ordained in Naples in 1572. Accused of heresy, he left the Order and travelled through Europe. He attacked the Church on various occasions. His principal errors consisted of defending that Jesus Christ is not God but a magician, that the Holy Spirit is the soul of the earth, and that the devil will be saved. Denounced to the Inquisition in Venice, he was condemned and burned in Rome.

Such is the general outline regarding the new "martyrs" who could be pronounced on the occasion of the Millennium. Yet in the Encyclical *Ut unum sint,* Your Holiness does not restrict yourself to the declaration of "martyrs," that is, those who died by shedding their blood. There would be still other "saints" from the other confessions who ought to be acknowledged. In fact, You affirm: "While for all Christian communities the martyrs are the proof of the power of grace, they are not the only ones to bear witness to that power. Albeit in an invisible way, the communion between our Communities, even if still incomplete, is truly and solidly grounded in the full communion of the saints – those who, at the end of a life faithful to grace, are in communion with Christ in glory. These saints come from all the Churches and Ecclesial Communities that gave them entrance into the communion of salvation. ....

"In the radiance of the 'heritage of the saints' belonging to all Communities, the 'dialogue of conversion' toward full and visible unity thus appears as a source of hope. This universal presence of the saints is in fact a proof of the transcendent power of the Spirit. It is the sign and proof of God's victory over the forces of evil which divide humanity. As the liturgy

---

Jan Hus (1369-1415) was ordained a priest in Prague (1400). Influenced by the writings of John Wyclif (1324-1384), even though they had been condemned by the Church, Hus translated them into the Czeck language and spread them, feeding the spirit of reform. He attacked Bishops and the Pope. He was excommunicated by the Archbishop of Prague, and the Pope placed his residence under interdict. He went to the Council of Constance to defend his doctrine and there he was judged, condemned, and burned.

See Gilles Lapouge, "Papa pretende beatificar Girolamo Savonarola," in *O Estado de S. Paulo,* 5/25/97; L. Accattoli, "Savonarola beato al Giubileo," in *Corriere della Sera,* 2/17/96; *Corriere della Sera,* "Il Cardinale Piovanelli: fate santo Savonarola," 12/6/95; "Il supplizio di Giordano Bruno: la Chiesa fa mea colpa," 11/15/96; "Savonarola verso la beatificazione a 500 anni dal rogo," 1/26/97; Cesare Medali, "Savonarola, martire o contestatore?" in *Corriere della Sera,* 2/3/97.

sings: 'You are glorified in your saints, for their glory is the crowning of your gifts.'"[20]

Once again, Your Holiness categorically affirms that the other religious confessions, different from the Catholic Church, are a normal and legitimate means to salvation – even to the point that they can have members who can be called "saints." Thus it could happen that the saints of tomorrow would be those very persons who until today were considered by Catholics as abettors of schism and heresy. This would be proclaimed by the Successor of Peter, in union with leaders of the other religions, at the passing of the Millennium.

Based on this, it seems licit to raise some hypotheses. Would such authorities begin by declaring the leaders of the Eastern Schism to be "saints"? In this case, would Photius and Michael Cerularius[21] be included in this number? So it seems, since a solemn joint declaration was read simultaneously at the Basilica of St. Peter by Paul VI and in Constantinople by Athenagoras I (12/7/65). While it claimed to revoke "the sentence of excommunication leveled against the patriarch Michael Cerularius" in 1054, the act had no practical effect. The passing of the years has shown that, despite the intentions of Paul VI and Athenagoras, the act was *de facto* considered ineffectual because it did not change the situation. The act pompously enti-

---

[20] John Paul II, *Ut unum sint*, no. 84.

[21] **Photius**, patriarch of Constantinople in the ninth century, broke officially with Rome, refusing to submit to her discipline on two occasions between 868 and 886. This was considered the origin of the dispute that two centuries later caused the Eastern Schism.

Michael Cerularius, patriarch of Constantinople from 1043 to 1058, had problems with Rome from the beginning of his rule and clashed several times with Sovereign Pontiff St. Leo IX. The last of these disputes resulted in the sentence of excommunication that the papal delegate, Cardinal Humbert Moyenmoutier, Bishop of Silva Candida, left on the altar of the Basilica of Saint Sophia in the year 1054. Since this time, the followers of Cerularius have been schismatics.

tled "the lifting of the excommunications" *de jure* meant nothing, since an excommunication only has validity in the Church
Militant while the accused is living. The *post-mortem* consequences are handed over to the judgment of God. Thus, the
lifting of the excommunication of Michael Cerularius was only
a diplomatic measure, without juridical effect or practical purpose.

Does not the new martyrology suggest something along
the lines of a rehabilitation of the abettors of the Schism? Will
the eventual aim be the rehabilitation of the two principal per-
petrators of the Schism? In this case, would Catholics have to
render honor to those who were the first to break the unity of
the Holy Church?

Or would the Holy See and the authorities of other religions begin by declaring less controversial persons to be
"saints"? The Russian Schismatic thinker Vladimir Soloviev,[22]
for instance, was praised in your Apostolic Letter *Fides et ratio*
as an example of a person who made "a philosophical inquiry

---

[22] **Vladimir Soloviev**, philosopher and Russian poet (1853-1900), was
an heir to "the French Revolution, German idealism, the Hegelian left
of Feuerbach and Marx, the positivism of Comte, the evolutionism of
Darwin, the doctrine of the super-man of Nietzsche, the arrogant
pessimism of Schopenhauer ... In him, the confessional dialogue took
on a world dimension and turned into dialogue between the East and
the West, between Byzantian-Moscow and Rome" (Hans Urs von
Balthasar, "Soloviev," in *La gloire et la Croix*, vol. II, Lyon: Aubier,
1972, pp. 167ff.). Soloviev defended the interior experience as the last
recourse to reach the Absolute. He thought that the future of
philosophy would be a synthesis between the philosophy of the West
and the theological doctrine of the East. In his work, traces of
pantheism have been found. He defended the idea of the union of
churches as the way to prepare for the unification of humankind and,
for this reason, he is considered the precursor of ecumenism. His
evolutionist cosmology of man approaches systems of thought of
various contemporary thinkers, notably that of Fr. Teilhard de Chardin,
SJ.

that was enriched by engaging the data of faith."[23] This, added to the indisputable prestige that he enjoys in circles of the *Nouvelle Theologie*, could stimulate his name to be proposed for the general veneration of Catholics, Orthodox, and Protestants.

It does not seem that the two hypotheses would exclude each other. Either the more or the less prominent Schismatics could, without difficulty, be presented as "saints."

Various events regarding the heresiarchs of Protestantism are also cause for pressing concern. Above, we cited the "lifting of the excommunication" of Cerularius (1965). Below, we record two statements of Cardinal Willebrands indicative of the times (1970, 1983) as well as two significant documents of Your Holiness (1983, 1984). They are not the most recent, undoubtedly, but they seem to reflect the base for the present reality: the exaltation of Luther, Zwingli, and Calvin.

Cardinal Jan Willebrands, then president of the Secretariat for Promoting Christian Unity, spoke of Luther in terms that Catholics usually reserve for St. Thomas Aquinas. The Angelic Doctor justly deserves the title of "common master" or "common doctor," which signifies that he should be respected by all of the theological schools in the Church. Yet Cardinal Willebrands praised Luther in his official speech at Evian in 1970 at the fifth plenary meeting of the Lutheran World Federation Council in Evian. Speaking about the doctrine of justification, the Cardinal applied to Luther the title of "common master," properly reserved for St. Thomas Aquinas. These were his words:

"Who cannot recognize that a more just assessment of the person and work of Martin Luther is imperative? Over the last few centuries, the person of Martin Luther has not always been duly respected by Catholics, and his theology has not always been correctly expounded. This has served neither truth nor

---

[23] John Paul II, Encyclical *Fides et ratio*, of November 15, 1998, in *Origins,* 10/22/98, vol. 28/19, no. 74.

love, and therefore, it has not served the unity that we strive to achieve between ourselves and the Catholic Church. On the other hand, we can happily say that in the last few decades Catholic scholars have been striving for a more precise understanding of the figure of Martin Luther and his theology .... Today, who would dare to deny that Martin Luther was a profoundly religious personality who sought the message of the Gospel honestly and with abnegation? Who could deny that in spite of the torments he inflicted upon the Catholic Church and the Holy See – truth demands that we speak out – he preserved a considerable measure of the riches of the ancient faith? Did not Vatican Council II approve demands that had been formulated by Martin Luther? And, by these, are not many aspects of the Christian faith and life better expressed today than in the past? To say this .... is a reason for great joy and hope.

"In an extraordinary way for his time, Martin Luther made the Bible the starting point of theology and Christian life. In your churches, the Bible has since enjoyed a privileged place and has been studied with great zeal. For its part, with a profundity never before attained, Vatican Council II inserted the Holy Scripture – which has always been a treasure in the Catholic Church – more fully into the life of the Church and its members and made it more fruitful for the latter .... In Martin Luther, one word continuously repeats itself, the great word 'faith.' Luther profoundly recognized its value, and many men, both inside and outside your churches, have learned to live from it even to our day. If there seems to have been a certain exclusiveness on this point that might be derived from the emphasis that Luther gave it in his talks, the joint research by Catholic and Protestant scholars on this matter shows that the word 'faith' in the sense that Luther attributed to it certainly does not exclude works, love, and hope. One can properly say that, as a whole, Luther's notion of faith means nothing but what the Church calls love.

"It is neither necessary nor possible to expound here the essential points of Luther's theology. Many things would have to be said about his theology of the cross, his Christology, his insistence on the divinity of Christ, questions that today particularly unite us to him. Yet both Catholic and Protestant scholars draw our attention to still another matter: the difficulty of presenting the thinking of Luther precisely, exhaustively, and above all, proportionately, giving full justice to many of his formulations that he did not express in a systematic way.

"For me it is a pleasure to think that in this regard we agree with your sentiments .... In a session whose theme is *Sent to the World*, it is good to reflect upon a man for whom the doctrine of justification[24] was the *articulus stantis et cadentis Ecclesiae* [the turning point of the enduring Church]. He can be our common master in this field as he states that God must

---

[24] In its *Decretum de justificatione* of January 13, 1547, the Council of Trent dealt with the topic of the Protestant doctrine of justification (generically praised by Cardinal Willebrands). It pronounced anathema the errors of Luther and his followers in 33 canons. For example, these Lutheran theses were condemned by canons 9 to 12:

- "Can. 9. If anyone shall say that by faith alone the sinner is justified, so as to understand that nothing else is required to cooperate in the attainment of the grace of justification, and that it is in no way necessary that he be prepared and disposed by the action of his own will; let him be anathema" (D 819, cf. 798, 801, 804).
- "Can. 10. If anyone shall say that men are justified without the justice of Christ by which He merited for us, or that by that justice itself they are formally just: let him be anathema" (D 820, cf. 798f.).
- "Can. 11. If anyone shall say that men are justified either by the sole imputation of the justice of Christ, or by the sole remission of sins, to the exclusion of grace and charity, which is poured forth in their hearts by the Holy Spirit and remains in them, or even that the grace by which we are justified is only the favor of God: let him be anathema" (D 821, cf. 799ff., 809).
- "Can. 12. If anyone shall say that justifying faith is nothing else than confidence in the divine mercy which remits sins for Christ's sake, or that it is this confidence alone by which we are justified; let him be anathema" (D 822, cf. 792, 802).

continuously remain the Lord and our most essential human response must be an absolute confidence in and worship of God."[25]

Cardinal Willdebrands' acclaim of Luther could lead one to think that his name might soon be proposed as a "saint" of the new martyrology. But the Cardinal goes even further in his praises. In a speech at the Ecumenical Institute of Bari, he judged that for the Church to be cured of the "wounds of her past," She needed to make a "more just and honest portrait of Luther." Cardinal Willebrands spoke these words at a meeting commemorating the fifth centenary of the birth of the heresiarch (1983): "It cannot be denied that Luther is present in Western Christendom. His name is a sign of division within it. Hence the question, 'But why?' We can draft a quick answer, but the essential question remains: What is the deepest meaning of what happened? Is it sufficient for us to take refuge in the inscrutable mystery of Divine Providence? Or should we instead ask ourselves: What can we do today to heal the wounds of the past? And how should we do it? Making a more just and honest portrait of Martin Luther will also serve to heal the sufferings of the Body of Christ."[26]

In his speech at Bari, Cardinal Willebrands revealed the Catholic post-conciliar stance of adaptation to Protestantism: "In addition to recovering the central role of Scripture in the Church and the lives of the faithful, since Vatican II Catholics have been increasingly willing to reassess the common priesthood of the faithful and the co-responsibility of laymen in the whole life of the Church; to recognize the character of the

---

[25] Jan Willebrands, "Lecture delivered at the 5th Assembly of the Lutheran World Federation," 6/15/70, in *La Documentation Catholique*, 1569, 9/6/70, pp. 765f.

[26] J. Willebrands, Speech about Luther at the St. Nicolas Institute, apud Salvatore Manna, published under the title: "Il Card. Willebrands inaugura il corso dell'Istituto S. Nicola," in *L'Osservatore Romano*, 2/5/84, p. 6.

Pilgrim Church on earth; to reevaluate local churches, to accept liturgical reform with the introduction of national languages; to concede to having Communion under two species and the declaration of religious liberty."[27]

Would these conclusions be those only of Cardinal Willebrands? They seem to suppose the at least implicit assent of Your Holiness. This could be assumed even by the position of the Cardinal as president of the Secretariat for Promoting Christian Unity. If You disagreed with the stands of this Prelate, You would certainly have given him some warning. This pontifical silence alone would suffice it to be said that the Pope agreed with these policies and eulogies. Such silence would be an indirect but cogent proof.

There is, however, a direct and indisputable proof. It is your personal letter to Cardinal Willebrands encouraging and directing him to participate in the commemorations held on that occasion. You began the letter paying homage to the heresiarch by calling him "Doctor," which brings to mind the title of "common doctor" that Cardinal Willebrands employed for Luther. These were your words: "November 10th is the 500th anniversary of the birth of Doctor Martin Luther of Eisleben. On this occasion, numerous Christians .... remember that theologian who .... contributed substantially to the radical change of ecclesiastical and secular reality in the West. Until today our world feels his great impact on History."[28]

Your Holiness gave a certain imperative tone to the norms at the end of the letter to Cardinal Willebrands: "I trust, therefore, Honored Cardinal, that under your direction and on this foundation and in this spirit, the Secretariat for Promoting Christian Unity will carry forward this dialogue that began with

---

[27] Ibid.

[28] John Paul II, Letter to Cardinal Willebrands of October 83, published under the title, "La verità storica su Lutero alimenti il dialogo per l'unità," in *L'Osservatore Romano*, 11/6/83, p. 4.

such great seriousness in Germany even before Vatican Council II; and that you will do this with fidelity to the faith freely given, which implies penitence and a readiness to learn from listening."[29]

This "foundation" and "spirit" that You propose the Cardinal to adopt includes acknowledging a "fraternity" with Protestants and affirming Luther's "profound religiousity" and "ardent passion" for eternal salvation. This is quite evident from the following paragraphs of your letter: "Well-known personalities and institutions of Lutheran Christendom have expressed the desire that the year dedicated to Luther be marked by a genuine ecumenical spirit and that reflections about Luther may contribute to the unity of Christians. I welcome this intention with satisfaction, seeing it as a fraternal invitation to achieve a more profound and complete vision of historical events and a critical analysis of Luther's multifarious heritage by means of this common effort. Indeed, the scientific research of evangelical and Catholic scholars, which has already led to many points of convergence, have made a more complete and nuanced picture of Luther's personality as well as a more complex interlacing of the historical, political, and ecclesiastical reality in the first half of the sixteenth century. These results have given visible proof of the profound religiousity of Luther, who was moved by an ardent passion for the question of eternal salvation."[30]

One cannot but be perplexed at finding Your Holiness extending "with satisfaction" a "fraternal invitation" to Protestants and overestimating historical and political circumstances in order to find many "points of convergence" between the Catholic Church and the Protestant heresy.[31]

---

[29] Ibid.

[30] Ibid.

[31] Although further on Your Holiness gives some importance to doctrinal controversy in the "dialogue" with Protestants, in this excerpt You

Regarding the errors of Luther, all of which involve matters of Faith, the sketch of "a more complete and nuanced picture of his personality as well as of the complex interlacing of historical reality" does nothing to change the solemn condemnation of the heresiarch's theses pronounced by Pope Leo X in the Bull *Exsurge Domine* of June 15, 1520. He summarizes this teaching with these strong words: "We condemn, reprove, and entirely reject each one and all of the aforementioned articles or errors [of Luther] as heretical, scandalous, false, offensive to pious ears, seductive of simple minds, and opposed to Catholic truth."[32]

Thus it is surprising to see You describe Luther as a man gifted with a "profound religiosity" and an "ardent passion" for

---

appear to subordinate the understanding of truth to historical conditions. In contrast with this tendency, consider the clear teaching of Saint Pius X condemning the Modernist errors in apologetics: "Hence that common axiom of the Modernist school that in the new apologetics controversies in religion must be determined by psychological and historical research" (Encyclical *Pascendi Dominici gregis*, of September 8, 1907, no. 35).

Further, the Decree *Lamentabili* of the Roman and Universal Holy Inquisition of July 3, 1907 presents a *Syllabus* of condemned Modernist propositions, some of which can be indirectly likened to your position. They include the following:

"3. From the ecclesiastical judgments and censures passed against free and more scientific exegesis, one can conclude that the Faith the Church proposes contradicts History and that Catholic teaching cannot really be reconciled with the true origins of the Christian religion ....

"22. The dogmas the Church holds out as revealed are not truths that have fallen from heaven. They are an interpretation of religious facts which the human mind has acquired by laborious effort ....

"54. Dogmas, Sacraments, and Hierarchy, both their notion and reality, are only interpretations and evolutions of the Christian intelligence which have increased and been perfected by an external series of additions to the little germ latent in the Gospel."

[32] Leo X, Bull *Exsurge Domine*, of June 15, 1520, in DS 1492.

eternal salvation, which would contradict the perennial teaching of the Church.

One sees that Cardinal Willebrands, whose statements and participation in the ceremonies commemorating the birth of the heresiarch cause astonishment, was in fact only following the orientation of the Pope, clearly laid out in the letter we have just cited.

When Your Holiness was in Germany in 1996, the possibility of absolving Luther was the subject of frequent conversation. For example, a typical news report stated: "Pope John Paul II is arriving in Germany today for a three-day visit. Bishop Karl Lehmann revealed yesterday that the Catholic Church and the Lutheran Church had reached an agreement to invalidate the mutual condemnations dating from the 16th century: 'The Pope will speak important words about this agreement, and I believe that we can expect surprises.' Vatican sources affirm that the Pope could revoke the condemnation of the father of the Protestant Reformation, Martin Luther."[33]

Another newspaper report explained why this absolution would not take place: "During his visit to Germany, Pope John Paul II intended to revoke the excommunication of Luther .... but he was dissuaded by advisers in face of the negative reaction of the German Episcopate, according to the weekly *Focus*. This historical initiative, which would have been made in the name of ecumenism, would have coincided with the 450th anniversary of the birth of Luther and been announced at the castle of Wartburg, where he took refuge during the religious wars between the Reform and the Counter-reformation."[34]

Such eulogies of Luther have continued into our days. For example, these were your words during your 1996 visit at the beginning of an ecumenical celebration in the city of

---

[33] "Papa tenta aproximação com protestantes alemães," in O *Estado de S. Paulo*, 6/21/96.

[34] "Papa pretendia reabilitar Lutero," in *Jornal do Brasil*, 6/16/96.

Paderborn: "After centuries of alienation and opposition, his [Luther's] memory permits us today to recognize more clearly the great importance of his request for a theology close to Sacred Scripture and a spiritual renewal of the Church."[35]

To judge by such texts and reports, who could be surprised if the heresiarch were to be absolved on the occasion of the Millennium? Or even eventually pronounced a "saint"?

During a trip to Switzerland, Most Holy Father, You also visited the Federation of Protestant Churches in Kehrsatz. There, You admiringly referred to the supposed "zeal" of Zwingli and Calvin: "This year we recall the zeal that animated two outstanding religious personalities in Swiss history: one, Huldrick Zwingli, whose fifth centennial you are commemorating with celebrations honoring his person and work; the other, John Calvin, who was born 475 years ago."[36]

Here as well, attributing zeal to Zwingli and Calvin can only be understood as a eulogy. Would this mean that the two heresiarchs could also be included in the new martyrology? It is a possibility that we sincerely hope will not take place.

Similar questions could be made about the rest of your speech, in which You reaffirmed your ecumenical commitment to "repair the damage" caused by the Catholic struggle against Protestants. Its leaders – in this case, Zwingli and Calvin – were supposedly moved by the noble intention of "making the Church more faithful" to Our Lord Jesus Christ: "Above all, the memory of events of the past should not limit our present efforts to repair the damage caused by those events. Cleansing the memory is an element of capital importance in ecumenical

---

[35] John Paul II, Speech given at a meeting with representatives of the evangelical church in Paderborn on June 22, 1996, in L. Accattoli, *When a Pope Asks Forgiveness*, New York: Alba House, 1998, p. 195.

[36] John Paul II, Speech to the Federation of Protestant Churches in Kerhsatz, on June 14, 1984, published under the title "La franca discussione degli avvenimenti storici, elemento fondamentale nel progresso ecumenico," in *L'Osservatore Romano*, 6/15/84, p. 8.

progress. It includes the frank recognition of reciprocal faults and errors committed in the reactions of one to the other, when each one had the intention of making the Church more faithful to the will of the Lord."[37]

If Calvin and Zwingli "had the intention of making the Church more faithful" to the will of Christ, would this indicate that they should be raised to the altar for the veneration of Catholics? It is a hypothesis that cannot be disgarded.

Therefore, Most Holy Father, the possibility exists that in the inauguration of the common martyrology, Catholics could be asked to renounce something that has been one of the characteristic marks of the Church for four centuries: its doctrinal opposition to Protestantism. And this Protestantism was personified by those very heresiarchs who founded some of its most important fragmentations.

Should this be true, one could say that for all practical purposes the common martyrology and the ecumenical festivities of the Millennium would have as a corollary the death of militancy in the Catholic Church.

3. Trip to Ur, Palestine, Israel, and Sinai

For a long time there has been talk about the Pope's trip to the East. The most probable route for the pilgrimage would be for Your Holiness to go to Iraq to visit the site of Ur in ancient Chaldeia, where Abraham set out to begin to fulfil his vocation. There, homage would be paid to the Patriarch, who is venerated by the three monotheist religions: Catholicism, Judaism, and Mohammedanism.

Afterward, following "in the footsteps of Abraham," the Pope would travel by way of Syria, Lebanon, Jordan, and Egypt to ancient Canaan, a territory being fought over today by the

---

[37] Ibid.

Jews and Arabs.[38] On the invitation of the Palestine Authority, Your Holiness would visit Bethlehem[39] and Jerusalem. This has been confirmed by your own words: "Jerusalem, with all its holy places that are also dear to the Hebrews and Muslims, is called to be the crossroads of peace and it cannot continue to be the cause of discord and division. I have great hopes that one day circumstances will permit me to go as a pilgrim to that unique city in order to relaunch from there, together with Hebrew, Muslim, and Christian believers, the message and charge of peace, which was already directed to the whole human family on October 27, 1986 in Assisi."[40]

It has been noted that Rome has already announced a new Assisi for 1999.[41] It hardly seems probable that there would be two meetings of the same kind, although this possibility cannot be completely excluded. Therefore, it will be considered in order to take this analysis to its full limits.

If this encounter were to take place in the Holy Land, could it become, by chance, a new ecumenical council like the one imagined by Cardinal Suenens? He has already raised this proposition as a hypothesis: "The star that guided the Magi Kings to Bethlehem already shines in the sky of ecumenism. Pilgrims of unity have set out again; the road is continuously filled with stones and the ways are uncertain; we are still crossing the desert. But, unlike the Magi Kings whose names come to us from the legends, today's pilgrims have well-known

---

[38] Marco Politi, "Sulle orme di Abramo," in *30 Giorni,* June 1998, p. 16.

[39] "Papa irá a Belém em 2000, diz Arafat," in *Folha de S. Paulo,* 12/20/96; "Convite palestino," in *O Estado de S. Paulo,* 6/13/98.

[40] John Paul II, Speech at the closing of the meeting of the Eastern Patriarchs, apud Luigi Accattoli, "Il Papa: Parlerò di pace a Gerusalemme," in *Corriere della Sera,* 3/1/91; Guido Moltedo, "Concluso il summit vaticano. Il Papa andrà a Gerusalemme," in *Il Manifesto,* 3/7/91; Joseph Vandrisse, "Jean-Paul II: Demain, à Jerusalem...," in *Le Figaro,* 3/7/91.

[41] See pp. 5ff.

names .... they are called Paul VI, Athenagoras, Ramsey I
know neither when nor where the decisive meeting will take
place. Will it be a Vatican III? Perhaps. But since in a dream
you can overcome all obstacles, why couldn't the final meeting
be in the same place that was the cradle of Christianity? Why
would the council of reconciliation not be a Second Council of
Jerusalem?"[42] Only time will tell if the Millennium is preparing
councils like this for us.

Further, plans have been announced for a meeting of
Your Holiness with Jewish and Muslim leaders on Mount Sinai
in order, according to some, "to mark the reconciliation of the
three major monotheist religions."[43] According to others, the
meeting would include these three religions along with the
Protestants and Orthodox."[44] Again, the question rises: Would
this be a new Assisi? A new ecumenical council?

4. A common declaration of "faith" in Ur, or on the top of Mount Sinai

The trip of the Pope to the East takes on special characteristics due to its historic significance. Abraham was father of
two races, the Hebrews and the Arabs, even though these two
peoples took different religious paths. The Hebrews, after denying Our Lord Jesus Christ, turned against the promise of their
own vocation and, in a certain way, even became hostile to it
(Rom. 3:27; 9:31; 11:7-10). The latter, after taking up the Muslim precepts, founded a new religion that did not coincide with
the first plans that God had showed them (Gen. 21:17-21).

---

[42] Leo Jòzef Suenens, "Alcuni compite della teologia oggi," in *L'avvenire della Chiesa - Il libro del Congresso*, Brescia: Queriniana, 1970, pp.
55-58.

[43] "Papa deve visitar Terra Santa no fim do milênio," in *O Estado de S.
Paulo*, 4/9/98.

[44] Marco Politi, "Duemila, giubileo di pace," in *La Repubblica*, 11/12/94.

Catholics also have Abraham as "the father of us all" for, as St. Paul affirms, we are the true children of the promise (Rom. 4:13-25; 9:8).

Thus, the pilgrimage of Your Holiness to this city takes on a symbolic meaning: it would be the acceptance of the *status quo* of the three religions linked to the Patriarch. Yet it is not clear how such an acceptance could be viable since among the three religions there are differences too great even to enumerate here: dogmatic, moral, disciplinary, canonical, liturgical, exegetical, etc.

One could ask: What do You, Most Holy Father, want to express symbolically by this visit to Ur and the rest of the pilgrimage? Would it be the abolition of all these differences? In this case, could a Pope repeal the differences that have remained invariable between the Catholic Church and Judaism for 2,000 years, and about 1,400 years for Mohammedanism? Could it mean that the Catholic Church would abandon the points that distinguish her from these false religions?

The aim of your visit to Bethlehem and Jerusalem also seems to be reconciliation. Undoubtedly, important diplomatic mediations could be made by the Pope in trying to resolve the complicated Arab-Israeli dissension over the disputed territory and, above all, over the *status* of Jerusalem.[45] Yet this would not seem to be the principal motive for your journey. Again one

---

[45] Archbishop Jean-Louis Tauran, Secretary of the Holy See for State Relations, spoke quite significantly about the status of Jerusalem: from the cultural point of view, it should be the patrimony of humanity; from the political point of view, it should be the capital of the Arabs and Jews. He said: "First of all, it [the Holy See] asks that Jerusalem be respected for what it is in itself or rather what it should be, compared with what it actually is. That is what I defined .... as the vocation or identity of the Holy City. Jerusalem is a treasure of all humanity .... I must add that there is nothing to prevent Jerusalem .... from becoming the symbol and the national center of both the peoples that claim it as their Capital" ("La Santa Sede e Gerusalemme," in *L'Osservatore Romano*, 10/26-27/98, p. 10).

returns, with deep concerns, to the perspective of the symbolism of these acts.

Similar commentaries could be made about the meeting planned for Mount Sinai. What could be the meaning of a common declaration of "faith" among the three monotheist religions except for the abdication of fundamental points of Catholic Doctrine?

5. Requests for Pardon

Much has been said about an examination of conscience and a correlated request for pardon that could be made on the occasion of the Millennium.

Unfortunately such requests for pardon have become almost routine in the time during and after the Council. Inspired by the doctrine that the Church would be "holy and sinning," or according to a more radical expression, "chaste and a prostitute,"[46] conciliar Popes have not been parsimonious in criticizing the past glory of the Holy Catholic Church.

---

[46] Regarding this progressivist idea that the Church would be both holy and sinning, or chaste and a prostitute, a few words of clarification may assist the Reader. Various heresies allege that the Catholic Church, to the measure that She has become powerful and the proprietor of earthly goods (sacred buildings, schools and hospitals, statues, art, etc.), She has allowed herself to fall into the state of sin. They defend a an impoverished, or "miserabilist" Church that supposedly would reflect more perfectly the evangelical ideals. Accusing the Catholic Church of sin, they then go on to impute to her other outrages, comparing her to a prostitute who has sold her honor for riches.

This double accusation, that the Church would be a sinner because of her wealth and power and the qualification of this supposed sin as prostitution has been taken up by important representatives of progressivist thinking. They have returned to this attack with certain adjustments, which do not atenuate the gravity of the offense, but at times augment and at other times avoid any immediate identification with the heretics of the past.

The first steps were taken by John XXIII when he decided to suppress the requests for the conversion of the Jews from the final prayers of the Mass. Later, he ordered that schismatics and heretics should no longer be labeled as such, but instead should be called our "separated brethren."
At the opening of the second conciliar session of September 29, 1963, Paul VI asked pardon of our "separated brethren": "We speak now to the representatives of the Christian denominations separated from the Catholic Church, who have nevertheless been invited to take place as observers in this solemn assembly .... If we are in any way to blame for this sepa-

---

First, such progressivists point not only to the material power of the Church, but also to her juridical and institutional power as a sin (Yves Congar, *"Pour une Église servante et pauvre,"* Paris: Cerf, 1963, pp. 107-123). They have even identified it as the sin of "phariseeism," which would be the hypocritical observance of the letter of religious or moral law without regard for the spirit and would make the juridical system an end in itself (Y. Congar, *"Vraie et fausse réforme dans l'Église,"* Paris: Cerf, 1950, pp. 152-170). It further defines this in doctrinary form as the 'sin of the Synagogue,' or the absolutization of transacted forms (Ibid., pp. 152ff., 170-195). The exercise of militancy, the combat of error and evil, would also be a sin for which the Church should make penance (Paul VI, Speech at the ecumenical ceremony at St. Paul Outside the Walls, of December 4, 1965, published under the title *Sacra funzione nella Basilica Ostiense per impetrare l'unita di tutti i cristiani,* in *Insegnamenti di Paolo VI,* Tipografia Poliglotta Vaticana, vol. III, 1965, p. 698).

Second, sin is attributed not only to the members of the Church, but to the the Divine Institution itself (Karl Rahner, "La Chiesa peccatrice nei decreti del Vaticano II," Rome: Paoline,1968, pp. 452, 465, 477; Hans Urs von Balthasar, *Casta meretrix,* in *Sponsa Verbi,* Brescia: Morcelliana, 1969, passim).

About the doctrine of the Church as holy and sinning, see also A. Sinke Guimarães, *In the Murky Waters of Vatican II,* Rockford, IL: TAN, 1999, 2nd ed., Chapter 7, no. 3, §§ 20-28.

With regard to Catholic Doctrine, which does not admit sin in the Church, see the teaching of the Sovereign Pontiffs Gregory XVI and Pius XI in Chapter II, p. 44.

ration, we humbly beg God's forgiveness and also ask pardon of our brethren who feel themselves to have been injured by us."[47]

Paul VI made other pronouncements along these lines. The most significant seems to be at the "lifting of the excommunication" of Michael Cerularius, which has already been mentioned. On this occasion, he said: "We affirm, before the Bishops who have come together at Ecumenical Council Vatican II, that we feel a lively sorrow for the words spoken and the gestures made in that time which cannot be approved. We desire, moreover, to remove and cancel from the memory of the Church and to bury completely in the memory of time the sentence of excommunication that was imposed in that epoch."[48]

In the conciliar documents there are also open doors to requests for pardon and the notion of the "sinning Church." Among so many, these are a few of the most characteristic examples.

First, the Constitution *Lumen gentium* makes this affirmation: "The Church, embracing sinners in her bosom, is at the same time holy and always in need of being purified, and incessantly pursues the path of penance and renewal" (LG 8).

Second, the Decree *Unitatis redintegratio* declares this: "From her very beginnings there arose in this one and only Church of God certain rifts which the apostle strongly censures as damnable. But in subsequent centuries more widespread disagreements appeared and quite large Communities became separated from full communion with the Catholic Church – developments for which, at times, men of both sides were to blame" (UR 3).

---

[47] Paul VI, Opening Speech of the Second Conciliar Session, apud Luigi Accattoli, *When the Pope Asks Forgiveness*, p. 22.

[48] Paulo VI, Brief *Ambulate in dilectione*, of December 7, 1965, in *Insegnamenti di Paolo VI*, 1965, p. 734.

Third, the Declaration *Nostra aetate* takes no account of the 2,000-year religious opposition between the Catholic Church and Judaism, but acts as if the antagonism stemmed from racial prejudices. It says: "The Church repudiates all persecutions against any man. Moreover, mindful of her common patrimony with the Jews, and motivated by the gospel's spiritual love and by no political considerations, She deplores the hatred, persecutions, and displays of anti-Semitism directed against the Jews at any time and from any source" (NA 4).

However, with respect to requests for pardon, no one has been more prodigious than Your Holiness. Although many examples could be given, it suffices to cite here some statements.

The document *Reflections on the Great Jubilee of the Year 2000* was addressed to the Cardinals and became the base for the Apostolic Letter *Tertio millennio adveniente*. In it, recalling the study about Galileo, You asserted: "A close look at the history of the second millennium can perhaps provide evidence of other similar errors or even faults as regards respect for the autonomy due the sciences. How can we be silent about so many kinds of violence perpetrated in the name of the Faith? Religious wars, courts of the Inquisition, and other violations of the rights of the human person."[49]

Yet among the principal preachers of the Crusade – indisputably a war of religion – we can count Blessed Urban II and St. Bernard of Clairvaux. Among the avid supporters of the Inquisition figures St. Dominic of Gusman. And St. Pius V was one of the most illustrious inquisitors. However, according to your criteria, these Saints would have to be included among those accused of the crimes noted above. How can such a contradiction be resolved? Should Catholics, in order to remain faithful, condemn the saints of the past and the glorious Catholic militancy in defense of the Faith? Or should they view with a

---

[49] John Paul II, "Reflections on the Great Jubilee of the Year 2000," apud L. Accattoli, op. cit., p. 57.

certain caution those who today condemn the saints and praise the heretics? These are questions for which we ask the favor of a clear and secure orientation.

Your Holiness would also seem indisposed toward Catholic militancy in the following excerpt: "As the second millennium of Christianity already draws to a close, the Church should become more fully conscious of the sinfulness of her children, recalling all those times in History when they departed from the Spirit of Christ and his Gospel and, instead of offering to the world the witness of a life inspired by the values of faith, indulged in ways of thinking and acting which were truly forms of counter-witness and scandal."[50]

Even though this phrase may seem generic, one understands from its context that an allusion is being made to Catholic intransigence and its consequent combativity.

With respect to the Catholic wars, Your Holiness has been decided in condemning them. At the canonization of Jan Sarkander, a martyr killed by the Moravian Protestants, You found occasion to ask pardon indirectly for the armed fight in defense of the Faith: "Today, I, Pope of the Church of Rome, in the name of all Catholics, ask forgiveness for the wrongs inflicted on non-Catholics during the turbulent history of these peoples; at the same time, I pledge the Catholic Church's forgiveness for whatever harm her sons and daughters suffered."[51]

The Holy Inquisition does not escape the critique of Your Holiness: "Another painful chapter of History to which the sons and daughters of the Church must return with a spirit of repentance is that of the acquiescence given, especially in certain centuries, to *intolerance and even the use of violence* in the service of truth .... Yet the consideration of mitigating factors

---

[50] John Paul II, Apostolic Letter *Tertio millennio adveniente*, in *L'Osservatore Romano*, 11/14-15/1994, supplement, no. 33.

[51] John Paul II, "Homily for the canonization of Jan Sarkander," at Olomouc, 5/21/1995, apud L. Accattoli, op. cit., p. 146.

does not exonerate the Church from the obligation to express profound regret for the weaknesses of so many of Her sons and daughters who sullied her face, preventing Her from fully mirroring the image of her crucified Lord, the supreme witness of patient love and humble meekness."[52]

The sentence that Your Holiness launched against the Holy Inquisition is grave and rigorous, especially when we know that You have made so much effort to find extenuating circumstances for the errors and heresies that the Church has always fought. In contradiction to this, many scholarly secular studies are reevaluating in a more positive light the role carried out by the Inquisition.[53] To deny to Catholics the right to defend the Faith placed at risk is to sentence the Church to defeat and infiltration by her enemies. The condemnation of Your Holiness of the legitimate defense of the Faith would be equivalent to the doctor who, as absurd as it might be, would work against the instinct of conservation normal in every healthy body.

---

[52] John Paul II, *Tertio millennio adveniente*, no. 35.

[53] Marian T. Horvat, "The Holy Inquisition: Myth or Reality," Catholic Family News, March 1998, vol. 5, no. 3; John Tedeschi, *The Prosecution of Heresy: Collected Studies on the Inquisition in Early Modern Italy*. Medieval and Renaissance Texts and Studies, vol. 78, Binghampton, NY: 1991, pp. XI-XIV, 7-9; Denis Fahey, *The Kingship of Christ*, 3rd ed., Palmdale, Ca: 1990, pp. 40s.; Edward Peters, *Inquisition*, New York, London: 1988, pp. 52-57; Richard Kieckhefer, "The Office of Inquisition and Medieval Heresy: The Transition from Personal to Institutional Jurisdiction," *Journal of Ecclesiastical History*, January 1995, 46, p. 59.

These studies all examine and expose the "myth" of the Inquisition, which today serves as prextext for so many exaggerations. Dr. Horvat, for example, notes: "As Edward Peters points out so well in his landmark study *Inquisition,* 'the Inquisition' was an 'invention' of the religious disputes and political conflicts of the sixteenth century. 'It was later adapted to the causes of religious toleration and philosophical and political enlightenment in the seventeenth and eighteenth centuries. This process, which was always anti-Catholic and usually anti-Spanish, became universalized.'"

Given these examples, it could well be the case to appraise what new types of condemnation of Catholic militancy and what new requests for pardon Catholics might hear at the passing of the Millennium. All indications point to a broad request that would include the following: pardon for the past militancy of the Church, pardon for the Inquisition, pardon for the punishment of heretics, pardon for the doctrinal combat against the Jewish religion, etc. The only thing lacking seems to be to ask pardon for the existence of the Catholic Faith that stood so strongly against the other religions and that inspired the attitudes that are condemned today.

In the end, even this would not seem to be excluded from the panorama. Indeed, the most disconcerting example of a request for pardon is that which the Pope made regarding the Petrine Primacy. These are your words: "As I acknowledged on the important occasion of a visit to the World Council of Churches in Geneva on June 12, 1984, the Catholic Church's conviction that in the ministry of the Bishop of Rome She has preserved, in fidelity to the Apostolic Tradition and the faith of the Fathers, the visible sign and guarantor of unity, constitutes a difficulty for most other Christians, whose memory is marked by certain painful recollections and events. To the extent that we are responsible for these, I join my Predecessor Paul VI in imploring pardon."[54]

The generic request for pardon, made so soon after the description of the Petrine Primacy, gives the impression that there might be some error in this doctrine. Yet this prerogative of the Pope is solidly established on a dogmatic foundation. Could it be that the defense of this foundation produced the "painful recollections" that live in the memories of the heretics and schismatics for which Your Holiness "implored pardon"? Such generic accusations are very serious because they touch upon the whole of this crucial matter.

---

[54] John Paul II, Encyclical *Ut unum sint*, no. 88.

Therefore, a generic request for pardon about the Papacy would seem to deny the doctrine of the Petrine Primate, which would be contrary to dogma. How can such an act of humility be understood to conform to Catholic Doctrine?

Such would be the facts that would seem useful to view objectively the program that the Vatican and press organs are presenting for the festivities of the Millennium.

* * *

CHAPTER II

CATHOLIC DOCTRINE AND ECUMENISM

Most Holy Father, an important topic will be presented here for your consideration: the conformance between the ecumenical[55] and inter-religious initiatives of the conciliar Church,

---

[55] The Greek word *oikoumenikos* from which ecumenism derives signifies that which extends throughout the whole world, what is universal. In a certain way it is synonymous with the Greek word *katholikos*, which also means universal. This is the legitimate meaning of ecumenism. It is what strives for the true Faith to spread throughout the world, which was the missionary ideal as the Church understood it up to Vatican Council II.

This good ecumenism rests on several presuppositions: *First,* that the Catholic Faith is one and cannot be fragmented into smaller parts that would contain incomplete, but acceptable, pieces of the truth. This is expressed in the adage, *"bonum ex integra causa, malum ex quocunque defectu."* *Second,* it presupposes that the Holy Church is the only means by which one can achieve eternal salvation. On this basis, the Catholic Church has always taught that seeking the conversion of heretics, schismatics, Jews, and pagans was one of her principal objectives. It is one of her Catholic marks, and, in that sense, ecumen- ical in the sound sense of the word.

However, the ecumenism that is spoken of so much today in large part does not conform to this good ecumenism. Born from Protestant initiatives at the end of the last century that sought to draw in Catholics who tended toward relativism, this movement of "bad" ecumenism gained ground in liberal Catholic milieus and then in Modernist circles. After the strong anti-Modernist campaign of the pontificate of St. Pius X, it again took hold and acquired strength and influence up to its triumph at Vatican II in documents of major importance: the Decree

principally the Millennium festivities, and the uniform, constant, and universal teaching of the Catholic Magisterium. It is difficult to reconcile the teachings of the Pontifical Magisterium prior to Vatican II with the practical cooperation, diplomatic approaches, and even joint statements on doctrine that have become increasingly frequent from the reign of John XXIII until now.

Excerpts from teachings of the perennial Pontifical Magisterium will be reproduced here and then compared with what has been done in our days.

Pius IX, together with Vatican Council I, reiterated the immutable doctrine of the Church. Pope Pius IX taught that the Faith could be found only in the body of the Catholic Church and emphasized her separation from the false creeds. Contrary to this, numerous Prelates today are preaching some degree or other of parity of the Holy Church with other religions. Many examples of this could be given, but only these few will be cited for the sake of brevity.

Unitatis redintegratio, the Declaration *Nostrae aetate*, and the Declaration *Dignitatis humanae*.

This ecumenism departs from presuppositions diametrically opposed to those of true ecumenism: *First*, the Faith would no longer be one, but fragmented. What should be accepted is a "theological pluralism," in which each one would profess only parts of the truth and not the entire truth. *Second*, the Church should no longer strive to convert heretics, schismatics, Jews, and pagans from their false creeds, but should respect and adapt herself to them to the measure possible in search of a new "unity." This is an ecumenical unity that is founded upon relativism and religious syncretism, and tends toward a panreligion. This idea has been unanimously condemned by the Pontifical Magisterium up to Vatican II, as we shall see in this chapter.

For a further explanation of true and false ecumenism, see Plinio Corrêa de Oliveira, "Unperceived Ideological Transhipment and Dialogue," in *Crusade for a Christian Civilization*, vol. 12, no. 4, pp. 28f.; A. Sinke Guimarães, *In the Murky Waters of Vatican II*, Chap. IX, §§1f.

This is what Vatican I said about the difference between the Catholic Church and the false religions: "For to the Catholic Church alone belong all those many and marvelous things which have been divinely arranged for the evident credibility of the Christian Faith. But, even the Church itself by itself, because of its marvelous propagation, its exceptional holiness, and inexhaustible fruitfulness in all good works; because of its Catholic unity and invincible stability, is a very great and perpetual motive of credibility, and an incontestable witness of its own divine mission. By this it happens that the Church .... both invites to itself those who have not yet believed, and makes its sons more certain that the faith, which they profess, rests on a very firm foundation .... Wherefore, not at all equal is the condition of those, who, through the heavenly gift of faith, have adhered to the Catholic truth, and of those who, led by human opinions, follow a false religion."[56]

With exemplary force, Pius IX spoke about religious indifferentism, the essence of which today is called ecumenism and inter-religious dialogue. The condemnatory statement of the Pontiff is particularly cogent when he refers to those who "pretend that men can gain eternal salvation by the practice of any religion." The excerpts about the common martyrology (Chapter I, no. 2) seem to take as presupposed the exact opposite teaching. Yet Sovereign Pontiff Pius IX clearly stated: "Also perverse is the shocking theory that it makes no difference to which religion one belongs [religious indifferentism], a theory which is greatly at variance even with reason. By means of this theory, those crafty men remove all distinction between virtue and vice, truth and error, honorable and vile action. They pretend that men can gain eternal salvation by the practice of any religion, as if there could ever be any sharing between justice

---

[56] Pius IX in union with Vatican Council I, *Dogmatic Constitution on the Catholic Faith*, Session III of April 24, 1794, in D 1494.

and iniquity, any collaboration between light and darkness, or any agreement between Christ and Belial."[57]

It would thus not seem exaggerated to affirm that the first flagrant contradiction has appeared between two fundamental points of the Millennium festivities – the panreligious meeting and the common martyrology – and the traditional doctrine of the Church.

In the *Syllabus of Errors,* Pope Pius IX summarizes various teachings of his pontificate that are today generally passed over in silence. In it he condemns the 15th proposition: "Anyone is free to embrace and profess that religion which, guided by the light of reason, he judges to be true."[58] Likewise he condemns the 16th proposition: "In the cult of any religion, men can find the road of eternal salvation and achieve the same eternal salvation."[59]

How could the conciliar texts that state there is the possibility of salvation in the practice of innumerable religions be reconciled with the doctrine of Pius IX? Would not the hypothesis of a common martyrology be based on the error declared anathema by the 15th and 16th propositions of the *Syllabus* cited above? From this arises the embarrassing but inevitable question: Which would prevail: the doctrine taught by Pius IX, which conforms to the teaching of the Magisterium that preceded it, or that of Your Holiness, which was supported by Vatican II?

---

[57] Pius IX, Encyclical *Qui pluribus*, of November 9, 1846, in *The Papal Encyclicals 1740-1978*, vol. 1, ed. Claudia Carlen IHM, Raleigh: McGrath Publishing Co., 1981, p. 280.

[58] The same sentence is also condemned in the Apostolic Letter *Multiplices inter*, of June 10, 1851, and in the Allocution *Maxima quidem*, of June 9, 1862.

[59] The same thesis is condemned in the Encyclical *Qui pluribus*, of November 9, 1846, in the Allocution *Ubi primum*, of December 17, 1847, and in the Allocution *Singularem quidem*, of March 17, 1856.

Leo XIII's exposition of the changeless Catholic position of the defense of the Faith in face of heretics conflicts with the position of many today who say that such heretics are only partially, if at all, culpable for their errors. According to conciliar criteria, what should be more strongly emphasized are the points of Faith that the heretics already accept, to give the impression that they are close to achieving unity with the Church.

Contrary to this tendency, Leo XIII taught: "The Church, founded on these principles and mindful of her office, has done nothing with greater zeal and endeavor than She has displayed in guarding the integrity of the Faith. Hence She regarded as rebels and expelled from the ranks of her children all who held beliefs on any point of doctrine different from her own. The Arians, the Montanists, the Novatians, the Quartodecimans, the Eutychians, did not certainly reject all Catholic doctrine: they abandoned only a certain portion of it. Still who does not know that they were declared heretics and banished from the bosom of the Church? In like manner were condemned all authors of heretical tenets who followed them in subsequent ages: 'There can be nothing more dangerous than those heretics who admit nearly the whole cycle of doctrine, and yet by one word, as with a drop of poison, infect the real and simple faith taught by Our Lord and handed down by Apostolic tradition.'[60],[61]

The requests for pardon, ever multiplying as the Millennium nears, seem to assume that there would have been error and sin in the Catholic Church: She would be both "holy and a sinner."[62] As seen above, this faulty doctrine finds refuge in some of the documents of Vatican II.[63] And Your Holiness has

---

[60] *Tractatus de Fide Orthodoxa contra Arianos.*

[61] Leo XIII, Encyclical *Satis cognitum*, of June 29, 1896, in *The Papal Encyclicals*, vol. 2, p. 393.

[62] See note 46.

[63] See pp.32f.

also been the protagonist for many of these requests for pardon.[64]

Speaking in a diametrically opposed way, His Holiness Pope Gregory XVI asserted without hesitation this teaching: "Therefore, it is obviously absurd and injurious to propose a certain 'restoration and regeneration' for her [the Church] as though necessary for safety and growth, as if She could be considered subject to defect or obscuration or other misfortune."[65]

Another Pontiff, Pope Pius XI, affirmed this most beautifully: "During the lapse of centuries, the Mystical Spouse of Christ has never been contaminated, nor can She ever in the future be contaminated, as Cyprian bears witness: 'The Bride of Christ cannot be made false to her Spouse: She is incorrupt and modest. She knows but one dwelling, She guards the sanctity of the nuptial chamber chastely and modestly.'[66]"[67]

Thus, Most Holy Father, we ask a word of clarification: How can the teaching that the Church could be "holy and sinning," implied in passages of Vatican II, and the requests for pardon harmonize with the teachings of the two Pontiffs presented above?

Pope Pius XI analyzed the ecumenical efforts that were already beginning in his day and said that they "certainly can nowise be approved by Catholics": "For since they [those who strive to introduce a sentiment of universal fraternity into the Church] hold it for certain that men destitute of all religious sense are very rarely to be found, they seem to have founded on that belief a hope that the nations, although they differ among themselves in certain religious matters, will without much diffi-

---

[64] See pp. 30-37.

[65] Gregory XVI, Encyclical *Mirari vos*, in *The Papal Encyclicals*, vol. 1, p. 237.

[66] St. Cyprian of Carthage, *De Catholicae Ecclesiae unitate*, no. 6.

[67] Pius XI, Encyclical *Mortalium animos*, of January 6, 1928 in *Papal Encyclicals 1903-1939*, vol. 3, p. 317.

culty come to agree as brethren in professing certain doctrines, which form as it were a common basis of the spiritual life. For which reason conventions, meetings, and addresses are frequently arranged by these persons .... Certainly such attempts can nowise be approved by Catholics, since they are founded on that false opinion which considers all religions to be more or less good and praiseworthy .... Not only are those who hold this opinion in error and deceived, but also in distorting the idea of true religion, they reject it, and little by little, turn aside to naturalism and atheism, as it is called."[68]

The censure of Pius XI against today's partisans of ecumenism and inter-religious dialogue could not be more severe: "From which it clearly follows that one who supports those who hold these theories and attempt to realize them, is altogether abandoning the divinely revealed religion."[69]

Once again, we ask Your Holiness to address these critical discrepancies: How should this condemnation of Pius XI be understood with regard to the present day ecumenical initiative of the conciliar Church without causing a rupture? Did Pius XI and the Popes who preceded him err? Did the conciliar Popes err?

Further on, Pius XI refutes the sophism that ecumenism would be an expression of charity, established by the evangelical precept "ut unum sint" ("that they may be one"). Today, on the eve of the Millennium, this position has become widespread, and these very words have become the title of one of your encyclicals. Yet Pius XI clearly stated: "And here it seems opportune to expound [upon] and to refute a certain false opinion, as well as that complex movement by which non-Catholics seek to bring about the union of the Christian churches depends. For authors who favor this view are accustomed, times almost without number, to bring forward these words of Christ: 'That they all may be one .... And there shall be one fold and one shepherd,' with this

---

[68] Ibid., pp. 313f.

[69] Ibid.

signification however: that Christ Jesus merely expressed a desire and prayer, which still lacks its fulfillment. For they are of the opinion that the unity of faith and government, which is a note of the one true Church of Christ, has hardly up to the present time existed, and does not today exist ....

"They add that the Church in itself, or of its nature, is divided into sections; that is to say, that it is made up of several churches or distinct communities, which still remain separate, and although having certain articles of doctrine in common, nevertheless disagree concerning the remainder; that these all enjoy the same rights .... Controversies therefore, they say, and long-standing differences of opinion which keep asunder till the present day the members of the Christian family, must be entirely put aside, and from the remaining doctrines a common form of faith drawn up and proposed for belief, and in the profession of which all may not only know but feel that they are brothers .... This then is what is commonly said .... They soon, however, go on to say that that Church [the Roman Church] has also erred, and corrupted the original religion by adding and proposing for belief certain doctrines that are not only alien to the Gospel, but even repugnant to it. Among the chief of these they number that which concerns the Primacy of jurisdiction, which was granted to Peter and to his successors in the See of Rome."[70]

Your Holiness has asked Catholic and non-Catholic theologians to restudy the future role of the Papal Primacy so that it will no longer be an obstacle to panreligious union.[71] Doesn't such a request directly counter this grave censure of Pius XI?

How can the journey of Assisi and the panreligious commemoration being prepared for the Millennium festivities be reconciled with the prohibitions of Pius XI? This Pontiff qualified the attitude that is being assumed today by much of

---

[70] Ibid., p. 315.

[71] John Paul II, Encyclical *Ut unum sint*, nos. 90, 95.

the conciliar Church as "indeed iniquitous": "It is clear that the Apostolic See cannot on any terms take part in their [interconfessional] assemblies, nor is it anyway lawful for Catholics to support or to work for such enterprises; for if they do so they will be giving countenance to a false Christianity, quite alien to the one Church of Christ.

"Shall We suffer, what would indeed be iniquitous, the truth, and a truth divinely revealed, to be made a subject for compromise? .... Is it possible that the object of faith should in the process of time become so obscure and uncertain, that it would be necessary today to tolerate opinions which are even incompatible one with another? If this were true, we would have to confess that the coming of the Holy Ghost on the Apostles, and the perpetual indwelling of the same Spirit in the Church, and the very preaching of Jesus Christ, have several centuries ago lost all their efficacy and use, to affirm which would be blasphemy."[72]

Once again, Holy Father, how can these doctrines that seem so contradictory be reconciled?

Further on, Pope Pius XI censured the word "pan-Christians." Yet this expression is being employed today in descriptions of some of the Jubilee Year events. For example, the interreligious meeting planned for October 1999 officially has been designated the "Pan-Christian Encounter." The questions arise: Has the meaning of the word pan-Christian altered? Or has the doctrine taught by a Pope in times past as legitimate and true now been changed?

In fact, Pius XI stated: "These pan-Christians who turn their minds to uniting the churches seem, indeed, to pursue the noblest of ideas in promoting charity among all Christians: nevertheless, how does it happen that this charity tends to injure faith? Everyone knows that John himself, the Apostle of love, ... altogether forbade any intercourse with those who professed a

---

[72] Pius XI, Encyclical *Mortalium animos*, p. 316.

mutilated and corrupt version of Christ's teaching: 'If any man come to you and bring not this doctrine, receive him not into the house nor say to him, God speed you.' For this reason, since charity is based on a complete and sincere faith, the disciples of Christ must be united principally by the bond of one faith. Who then can conceive a Christian federation, the members of which retain each his own opinions and private judgment, even in matters which concern the object of faith, even though they be repugnant to the opinions of the rest?"[73]

This same Sovereign Pontiff taught a doctrine whose direct application would lead one to consider today's partisans of ecumenism as advocates of Indifferentism and Modernism. He made this decisive statement: "How so great a variety of opinions can make the way clear to effect the unity of the Church We know not; that unity can only arise from one teaching authority, one law of belief, and one faith of Christians. But We do know that from this it is an easy step to the neglect of religion, or Indifferentism, and to Modernism, as they call it. Those, who are unhappily infected with these errors, hold that dogmatic truth is not absolute but relative, that is, it agrees with the varying necessities of time and place and with the varying tendencies of the mind, since it is not contained in immutable revelation, but is capable of being accommodated to human life."[74]

Pius XI closes his Encyclical prohibiting ecumenism and refuting, already in his time, the basic premises behind the interconfessional festivities that are being prepared for the near future: "So it is clear why this Apostolic See has never allowed its subjects to take part in the assemblies of non-Catholics: for the union of Christians can only be promoted by promoting the return to the one true Church of Christ of those who are separated from it, for in the past they have unhappily left it. To the one true Church of Christ, we say, which is visible to all and

---

[73] Ibid.

[74] Ibid., p. 317.

which is to remain, according to the will of its Author, exactly the same as He instituted it .... For since the Mystical Body of Christ, in the same manner as His physical body, is one, compacted, and fitly joined together, it were foolish and out of place to say that the mystical body is made up of members which are disunited and scattered abroad: whosoever therefore is not united with the body is no member of it, neither is he in communion with Christ its head."[75]

Therefore, Most Holy Father, after having considered the unchangeable doctrine of the Church in these excerpts from the ordinary and extraordinary Pontifical Magisterium, it becomes very difficult not to see a contradiction between what these documents have affirmed and what is being announced for the Millennium festivities. In effect, could it be possible to allow "pan-religious encounters" without incurring the severe censure made by the Roman Pontiffs cited above? How can the partisans of false Orthodox and Protestant religions, and even of the Jewish and Muslim confessions, eventually be declared "saints," as is supposedly being planned for a common martyrology? How can one imagine a common declaration of "faith" among the monotheist religions, when Mohammedanism and Judaism deny a large part of Catholic dogma? Finally, how can one ask pardon for the "errors" that the Holy Catholic Church would have committed in the past in her combat against schismatics, heretics, and pagans without implicitly denying her militant character and the incorruptibility of her divine nature, as well as incurring the pontifical condemnations cited above?

These are some of the questions that leave so many Catholics perplexed and for which we humbly and respectfully request the paternal guidance of Your Holiness.

*

---

[75] Idem, pp. 78f.

In summary, Most Holy Father, our affliction could be expressed in this way: If the prior teaching of the Church is not true, would the Church have erred in demanding adhesion to this doctrine as the expression of revealed truth and as a condition of salvation? If, on the contrary, such doctrine is true, how can the contradiction with what is being taught today be explained? If it becomes clear that the road chosen by the post-conciliar teaching is contrary to the time-honored Magisterium, then where is the Institution directed by Your Holiness heading? If it is not clear where this road is leading us, as so it seems today, what direction should the faithful adopt in such confusion? In view of such tragic and crucial contradictions, we come to the Vicar of Christ, begging your response to the question that rises: *Quo vadis, Petre?*

*   *   *

CHAPTER III

FAILURES IN THE INTERNAL DYNAMICS OF RELIGIOUS POLITICS

If such serious perplexities rise in the doctrinal sphere, the practical advantages achieved in the sphere of inter-religious initiatives are also open to dispute. It could even be said that far from showing any great harvest in the ecumenical field, as is often insinuated, glaring failures are evident as the scene unfolds before the eyes of an observer. What is presented here pretends to be no more than a *tour d'horizon*.

1. Picture of the Schismatic Churches: Lack of Union and Resentment

With regard to the schismatics,[76] the former problems of reconciliation were aggravated when the "Iron Curtain" fell. For

---

[76] Until Vatican II, the governing norm in the Catholic Church when speaking about the false religions was to exercise a reserve in employing the nonobjective names that these confessions frequently chose for themselves. Thus, with respect to schismatics, the Church called them exactly that or employed a restriction – "the so-called orthodox," or simply the "orthodox" in quotations to express a reserve. The same was done with regard to the "so-called Anglican Catholics." A similar norm was in place for the names of the "churches" adopted by the various false confessions. It was common to say "the so-called Anglican church," the "so-called Orthodox church," etc., leaving the title of the church in lower case. There could be nothing more coherent for

example, the Catholic Church in the Ukraine, with its five million members, constituted the largest "Church of silence" under the Communist yoke. Only four days after the fall of the Berlin Wall,[77] our valorous Ukrainian brothers in the Faith began to reacquire the churches that Stalin had stolen from the Catholic Church and handed over to the subservient Orthodox church. This started a chain reaction, with the return of hundreds of churches to their legitimate owners. Innumerable members of this schismatic confession thus had the opportunity to return to the true religion: conversions to Catholicism numbered in the thousands.[78]

Often, after the return of churches to the Catholics, entire parishes converted, priests along with parishioners. This movement soon threatened a veritable hemorrhage for the Schism. A meeting of a Vatican delegation with Ukrainian Catholic and Russian Orthodox representatives ended in disaster. The Ukrainians stated that the Holy See delegates were favoring the Orthodox to the detriment of the Catholics.[79] Your Holiness had already recommended "humility, meekness, and patience" be

---

anyone who is convinced that the only true Church is the Catholic Church, which means She possesses the only possible orthodoxy.

With the Council, these norms were set aside. Innumerable religious confessions were called Churches and their beliefs were admitted as legitimate expressions of faith. Because of this, the old forms were virtually abolished. Today few even know of their prior existence.

In the present document, the author has adopted the norms in use up to Vatican II, taking care at times to maintain the more familiar usages so that his exposition is clear.

[77] Domenico del Rio, "Il Papa ai Vescovi tedeschi 'Un momento emozionante,'" in *La Repubblica*, 11/14/89.

[78] These assertions will not be demonstrated here since they will be documented further on in the chapter.

[79] Marina Ricci, "Os anos do degelo," in *30 Dias*, August-September 1991, p. 27.

shown to the Ukrainian Bishops who were meeting in Rome.[80] In orienting their relations with the Orthodox church, You had asked the European Bishops to "cease every type of unsuitable proselytism, absolutely avoiding any temptation to violence or form of pressure."[81] Undoubtedly, this was an attempt to attend to the requests of the Orthodox. But it was difficult to contain the zeal of our Uniate brothers .... The Schismatic cupola came to adopt a position of rancorous resentment toward the Holy See. This position generated a crisis that endures even to this day. Below are some principal events that have marked the ecumenical tonus of our times.

* Alexis II, patriarch of the Russian Orthodox church, rejected the invitation of Your Holiness (10/11/91) to participate in the European Synod at the end of November of 1991. In a communication explaining this refusal, the Russian Church synod presented various grievances: The Ukrainian Catholics were using violence and extortion in their efforts to proselytize; the Holy See had closed its eyes to this fact; it would thus have instituted a "parallel missionary structure" without prior consultation; this "almost ostensive aggression threatens to become a war of religion." Because of this, the Schismatic synod would not participate in the Vatican meeting.[82] At the European Synod, the Orthodox representative present repeated the complaints of the Russian schismatics, adding other similar griev-

---

[80] Salvatore Mazza, "'Un Patriarca a Leopoldi' - La rechiesta al Papa, invitato in Ucraina," in *Avvenire*, 2/10/91.

[81] *L'Osservatore Romano*, 6/12/91, p. 5; "Da Papa Wojtyla un ap-pelo al dialogo religioso: 'Pace fra uniati e ortodossi,'" in *Corriere della Sera*, 6/12/91.

[82] *La Pensée Russe*, Declaration on the Special Assembly of the Synod of Bishops about Europe, Paris, 10/21/91; Luigi Accattoli, "Il Patriarcato di Mosca respinge l'invito del Papa al Sinodo," in *Corriere della Sera*, 10/12/91.

ances of the Serbian, Bulgarian, and Romanian schismatics.[83]
From the Orthodox churches "of almost all the Eastern capitals
came war cries against the 'intolerable Catholic invasion' into
Eastern Europe," an Italian paper reported.[84]

　* At Constantinople, the heads of the Schismatic
churches met to discuss their relations with the Catholic Church
(3/15/1992). The final document, approved unanimously, affirmed that the Uniates who were proselytizing in Russia, Romania, and the Mideast had become an insuperable obstacle to
ecumenism. The Orthodox leaders made the progress of theological "dialogue" contingent upon resolving this "problem."
Instead of a resolution, the rupture became definitive. Headlines
read: "Relations with the Vatican Become Extremely Tense,"
"The Trench that Separates the Orthodox and the Catholics Has
Become an Abyss."[85] In one assembly, the patriarch of Athens,
Seraphim, and the head of the Serbian church "spoke out
strongly for" an official rupture with Rome.[86]

　* In September of 1992, hostilities between the Catholics
and the Orthodox religious authorities of Greece broke out and
lasted for about two months.[87]

　* In a press interview (12/28/92), Cardinal Angelo Sodano, Secretary of State, responding to a question about the trip
of Your Holiness to Russia, stated that it "would depend upon
overcoming the egoism and resentments of our Orthodox broth-

---

[83] *L'Osservatore Romano*, 12/4/91, p. 4; L. Accattoli, "Roma tradisce il
Concilio," in *Corriere della Sera*, 12/4/91.

[84] Antonio Ferrari, "Fra ortodossi e Vaticano è guerra sull'Est Europa,"
in *Corriere della Sera*, 2/24/92.

[85] A. Ferrari, "La chiesa ortodossa contesta l'"agressione" degli uniati,"
in *Corriere della Sera*, 3/16/92.

[86] A. Ferrari, "Ortodossi-Vaticano: alla ricerca del dialogo perduto," in
Corriere della Sera, 3/15/92.

[87] Paolo Tonucci, "La Guerra del Peloponeso - Governo e ortodossi
uniti per emarginare i 'papisti,'" in *Avvenire*, 11/8/92.

ers."[88] In April of 1993, it was admitted that there was a "complete paralysis in ecumenical relations between the Catholics and the Orthodox church."[89]

* A council of the Russian Orthodox church took place in Moscow in November of 1994. In a 70-page statement, patriarch Alexis II accused the Ukrainians Catholics of "using aggressive methods, employing violence to occupy churches, and carrying out brutal actions." Further on, he stated that the "legalization of the Greek-Catholic Church had been accompanied by a massive violation of the rights of orthodox believers." This display of rancor toward Rome did not end there: "Since the beginning of the '90s, we have observed the attempts of Vatican diplomacy to act in Russia with the aim of strengthening the operations of the Catholic Church and ignoring the Orthodox church."[90]

* In January of 1995, Alexis II confirmed the crisis of ecumenism: "Today this theological dialogue [between Catholics and the Orthodox] unfortunately is almost defunct because of the serious problems caused by the proselytizing of the Uniates."[91] After praising the good will of the Catholic ecclesiastical leaders who had encouraged ecumenism, the head of the Russian church criticized the lack of grassroots support for the effort: "But, at base, this appeal is far from being accepted. In many places in the Ukraine, conflicts continue between the Greek-Catholic and Orthodox communities. The question of the

---

[88] Angelo Sodano, Interview granted to *La Stampa*, Turin, 12/28/92, apud Luigi la Spina, "Sodano: A Bósnia não é o Golfo," in *30 Dias*, January 1993, p. 19.

[89] Aleksej Judin, "O Catecismo do degelo," in *30 Dias*, April 1993, p. 20.

[90] Alexis II, Interview granted to Gianni Valente, published under the title: "Alexis: do comunismo à cultura," in *30 Dias*, January 1995, p. 25.

[91] Ibid., p. 20.

division of [church] properties is still not completely resolved."[92]

* In May of 1995 the Catholic Archbishop of Athens
Nicolas Foscolos, denounced the continued discrimination of
Catholics in Greece. Catholic officials cannot construct any
building without the permission of the Greek Orthodox authorities; restrictions have been placed on lay Catholics in schools,
the armed services, and even travel.[93]

* During a visit to Rome on the Feast of Ss. Peter and
Paul (6/29/95), Bartholomew I, the Orthodox patriarch of Constantinople, stated: "The Encyclical *Ut unum sint* of Pope John
Paul II of Rome still reveals the excessive pretensions of the
Bishop of Rome regarding the primacy and infallibility, even if
in an indirect way."[94] He called the tone of the encyclical "pa-
ternalistic."[95]

* In an interview granted in September of 1995, Alexis II
summarized the difficulties of ecumenism: "Unfortunately, in
relations between the Vatican and the Russian Orthodox church,
obstacles have been raised by the activities of Catholics in the
canonical territory of the patriarchate of Moscow. First, there
was the problem of relations between the Greek-Catholics (Uniates) and the Orthodox .... But there are other things that compli-
cate our relationship. For example, until today we have not
reached a satisfactory agreement on the Catholic missionary
projects in Russian territory .... I think that we need a meeting to
discuss these questions with a full development of our inter-

---

[92] Ibid., p. 21.

[93] E. Carlier, "Los católicos griegos están siendo humillados," *Palabra*,
Madrid, May 1995, p. 14.

[94] Bartholomew I, Interview granted to Gianni Valente published under
the title, "Testemunhas, ou seja, mártires," in *30 Dias*, September
1995, p. 67.

[95] "Il patriarca in trionfo," in *Corriere della Sera*, 6/28/95.

ecclesial relations. Until now, it has been impossible either to agree upon a time or place for such a meeting."

Alexis II also expressed reservations about the measures aimed at achieving the "ecumenical unity" proposed by Your Holiness in the Apostolic Letter *Tertio millennio adveniente* – that is, a meeting on Mount Sinai and a common martyrology.[96] He said: "Certainly it would be utopic to hope that in five years we could resolve all that has divided us for a thousand years .... As for the meeting of all the Christian leaders on Mount Sinai or in some other place, it would be ideal that this meeting should have more than a symbolic significance; it should be preceded by some type of concrete fruit of the drawing together of Christians. I do not know if Mount Sinai is the ideal place for this meeting (in my view it would be difficult from a technical perspective), but it could happen in some other holy place of Christendom. As for the common martyrology, I believe that the question should be examined with great caution so that the glorification of the martyrs of one Christian tradition should not be considered offensive by another."[97]

* The heads of all the Schismatic churches met on the Island of Patmos (9/24/95) to commemorate the 1900 years since St. John wrote the *Apocalypse* there. Faced with the possibility of the presence of the Pope at this meeting, the synod of the Greek Orthodox church stated that this would be "inopportune and inappropriate at the present moment." The press noted that this statement "is another sign that the season for an easy ecumenism has definitely ended."[98]

* In a speech to the Catholic Bishops in which he attacked the Petrine Primacy (12/14/95), Bartholomew I defended

---

[96] *Tertio millennio adveniente*, nos. 24, 37, 53.

[97] Alexis II, Interview granted to Giovanni Cubeddu published under the title, "A herança comum," in *30 Dias*, September 1995, p. 71.

[98] Gianni Valente, "Com o olhar fixo em Jesus," in *30 Dias*, September 1995, p. 62.

the collegiate form of government of the Schismatic church and suggested that the Pope use his power to impose upon the Catholic Church a regime of equality among the Bishops in the government of the Church.[99]

* In June of 1996, a commission of the Russian Parliament rejected an amendment to a 1990 law on religious freedom. The amendment was proposed by the patriarchate of Moscow and called for an interdict to be placed upon "foreign missionary activities" in Russia. In a counterproposal, the commission demanded the prior registration of foreign religious organizations. Patriarch Alexis responded by exhorting the Republics to adopt stricter local laws.[100]

* Alexis II did not reply to your invitation to meet in the Hungarian monastery of Pannonhalma (11/7/96). Your Holiness waited for him, but he simply did not appear.[101]

* At the 11th World Conference on Missions and Evangelization (12/3/96) that took place in Salvador (Bahia, Brazil), metropolitan Kirill de Smolensk, speaking in the name of the patriarchate of Moscow, described the proselytism in Central and Eastern Europe as "the ecumenical catastrophe of the last years of the 20th century." After the advent of political liberty in the countries of the East came the "intrusion of orders of foreign missionaries, who considered the ex-Soviet Union a vast missionary camp. They acted as if the Gospel had not been proclaimed here." He continued, "Unless boundaries are established, ecumenism and proselytism are incompatible." According to him, the kind of proselytism taking place would not only express an erroneous conception of missionary work, but it would assume all the connotations of an "invasion of a culture,

---

[99] Bartholomew I, Excerpts from his speech published under the title, "E se o Papa não protegesse a Tradição?," in *30 Dias*, April 1996, pp. 32f.

[100] "Par fax - Russie," in *L'Actualité Religieuse*, 6/15/96, p. 10.

[101] "Alessio II non vola a Pannonhalma," in *Corriere della Sera*, 9/8/96.

according to the old missionary schemata of colonization." Kirill affirmed that this "assault unleashed by the West" had two effects: It blocked the ecumenical process, and it made Christianity "lose credibility in face of a secularized society."[102]

  * An open letter signed by one hundred priests that circulated in the Orthodox parishes of Moscow denounced a reported plan orchestrated by the Vatican for Catholic expansion in Russian territory (12/21/96). This missionary plan was called a "threat to the very existence of the Orthodox church in Russia." The complaints were directed above all to the Orthodox priests and laymen involved in ecumenical initiatives with Catholics and accused them of being engaged in "crypto-Catholicism." The position of the signatories of the document was said to be shared by 136 Russian bishops.[103]

  * In January of 1997, a release from *Compass Direct*, an international press service based in the United States, noted that after the fall of Communism in Eastern Europe, the Orthodox church had tried "to consolidate its dominant position by attempting to restrict the liberty of the other confessions." According to the report, this took place not only in Russia, but also in Bulgaria and Romania.[104]

  * The organization *Human Rights Without Borders* expressed concern about the "anti-ecumenical climate" in Romania (3/15/97). It denounced the violent action of the schismatics who opposed returning churches taken under the communist government. It emphasized that the radicality of members of the lower clergy was paralyzing attempts for dialogue.[105]

---

[102] K. de Smolensk, Speech on the Missions, apud Alfio Filippi, "Patriarcato di Mosca - Chiesa accusata: denaro - Chiesa che accusa: proselitismo," in *Il Regno*, 2/15/97, pp. 108f.

[103] Gianni Valente, "Com quem está o Patriarca?" in *30 Dias*, February 1996, p. 26.

[104] Laurent Grzybowski, "Menaces sur la liberté religieuse," in *L'Actualité Religieuse*, 3/15/97, pp. 10f.

[105] "Par fax - Roumanie," 3/15/97, in *L'Actualité Religieuse*, p. 12.

* In March of 1997, Bartholomew I expressed reserve about the ecumenical movement, noting that it had deviated from its initial intent for unity and had been reduced to meetings that were no more than social gatherings. With regard to unity with Rome, Bartholomew tempered the ardor of those who were thinking that there could be a quick and full communion between the Catholics and the Orthodox.[106]

* In an interview of April 15, 1997, Belgium Cardinal Godfried Danneels affirmed: "I am personally concerned about Rome-Moscow, Rome-Athens, and Rome-Constantinople relations. I have a great esteem for patriarch Bartholomew. But what can he do with his four thousand [sic] faithful in Constantinople?"[107]

* In a homily delivered on his trip to Milan (5/17/97), Bartholomew I stated, "It behooves us not to ignore the serious division that exists [between Orthodox and Catholics] notwithstanding the desire for unity and to concentrate our attention on the superficial fact of reconciliation and friendship reborn at the level of human relations."[108] Bartholomew's speech wakened little hope that the Orthodox church of Constantinople would participate in the meeting in Graz (Austria). Similar refusals to dialogue were made by the Orthodox churches of Romania, Greece, and Georgia.[109]

* In May of 1997, the number of churches in the control of the Uniate Catholics was 2,049 of the 3,249 that they had possessed before the Catholic Church was dissolved by the Soviet

---

[106] Geoffroy de Turckheim, "Constantinople entre Genève et Rome," in *L'Actualité Religieuse*, 3/15/97, p. 15.

[107] Godfried Danneels, Interview granted to Francesco Strazzari under the title, "Danneels: il rischio delle chiese nazionali," in *Il Regno*, 6/15/97, p. 250.

[108] "Ecumenismo provato," in *Il Regno*, 6/15/97, p. 326.

[109] Ibid.; see also Gabriella Zucchi, "Bartolomeo I e la scuola di Ambrogio," in *Il Regno*, 6/15/97, p. 328.

power in 1946. Another 661 churches were designated for common usage, but in only 167 of these did this take place peacefully. The Pontifical Council for Christian Unity observed that in 408 cases, the Orthodox denied Catholics use of the churches, while in only 11 cases did the contrary take place.[110]

* In an official letter dated June 11, 1997, the Russian Orthodox synod released a terse statement saying that Alexis II would not participate in the meeting with Your Holiness in Vienna on June 21. Final arrangements for an ecumenical meeting in Graz were to be discussed there. The statement alleged that "several important conditions needed to make such a meeting fruitful are still lacking." The program had already been carefully planned by the Pontifical Council for Christian Unity, which had reached the point of fine tuning details regarding the site, program, and invitations. It had even drafted a joint statement proposed as the formal basis for the meeting. On May 20, Alexis sent an official letter to the Pope affirming that he would not appear. [111]

Attempting to justify this absence at the meeting and the consequent collapse of ecumenism, one press report noted: "The internal conditions in the Orthodox world and in its relations with Rome do not seem to be leading in the near future to a realization of the objective [of unity]. The actions of Bartholomew I and of Alexis II were strongly conditioned by public opposition to ecumenism by the Byzantine and Russian monasteries, as well as by the Russian and Greek episcopates."[112]

---

[110] "Encontro ecumênico católico-ortodoxo em Bari," in *30 Dias*, May 97, p. 43.

[111] Arthur DiNunzio, "Russia, Far from Unity," in *Catholic World Report,* August/September, vol. 7, no. 8; "Ecumenismo provato," in *Il Regno,* 6/15/97, p. 326; L. Accattoli, "No all'incontro con Wojtyla," in *Corriere della Sera,* 6/13/97.

[112] *Il Regno,* Ibid., p. 327.

* Bartholomew I did not send representatives to Rome on the occasion of the Feast of Ss. Peter and Paul (6/29/97). With this, he broke a tradition of 21 years of visits to the Eternal City by official delegations of the Orthodox patriarchs of Constantinople.[113]

* In August of 1997, Cardinal Franz König commented on the meeting that did not take place between Your Holiness and Alexis II. He made this description of the religious climate in Eastern Europe: "In 1989 there was a great anticipation [for ecumenical meetings]. A few months later, it had been concretely verified that this brick wall had fallen, only to be replaced by a much stronger one made of suspicion."[114]

* After the Russian State *Duma* passed the new law on religious freedom elaborated under the inspiration of the Russian Orthodox church, it was presented for the final approval of President Boris Yeltsin (7/22/97). The law restricted the rights of religious organizations with no documental proof of existence in Russia for fifteen years. Such organizations, which targeted the Catholic Church, would not have the right to distribute religious literature, to create their own religious institutes, or to publish newspapers and magazines; further, their members were prohibited from teaching in public schools. Yeltsin yielded to pressures from Alexis II to approve the bill. Faced with a strong international clamor, in which the voice of Your Holiness stood out, and the threat of financial sanctions, the President decided to veto the bill and return it to the *Duma*.[115]

---

[113] Gianni Valente, "O ecumenismo de quem tem a fé no coração," in *30 Dias*, November 1997, p. 30.

[114] Franz König, Interview granted to Gianni Valente, published under the title, "O humano e o divino na Igreja," in *30 Dias*, August-September 1997, p. 11.

[115] "El patriarca ortodoxo ruso pide a Yeltsin que firme la ley religiosa que el Papa criticó," in *ABC*, Madrid, 7/19/97; "EUA e Rússia se opõem por questão religiosa," in *Folha de S. Paulo*, 7/19/97; "EUA criticam

Despite this veto and Yeltzin's allegation that the bill violated human rights, Alexis II would not back down. Instead, he affirmed that the law "does not violate the rights of anyone, but cuts off passage to the pseudo-missionary and destructive forces that are inundating Russia and other countries of the former USSR."[116] Shortly after, Yeltsin sanctioned this law, and several days later it was adopted by the *Duma* (9/29/97). It imposed strict limits on all religious groups that were not recognized by the Communist regime. Anticipating the approval of this federal law, 26 of the 889 regions of Russia had already approved directives that restricted the activities of "non-traditional" religions.[117]

    * In November of 1997, a news commentator summarized the situation of the ecumenical movement in the Orthodox church: "Judging the symptoms seen in the last months, the ecumenical movement survives in a glacial state .... An impressive sequence of blows has toppled the residual ecumenical spirit, already undermined since 1989. Before the ecumenical European Assembly in Graz in June of this year, the Orthodox church of Georgia decided to leave two of the most important ecumenical groups (the World Council of Churches, which has 332 Christian Orthodox and Protestant member churches from around the world, and the Conference of European Churches, which brings together 115 Protestant and Orthodox churches on the continent).

    "There was also the last minute collapse of the meeting between John Paul II and Alexis II, orthodox patriarch of Mos-

---

Rússia e China por liberdade religiosa," 7/23/97; "Pressionado, Yeltsin veta lei que restringia religiões," 7/23/97.

[116] Rodrigo Fernandez, "El patriarca de la iglesia ortodoxa rusa compara al Catolicismo con la OTAN," in *El País*, Madrid, 7/26/97.

[117] David Filipov, "Católicos sofrem com nova lei russa," in *O Estado de S. Paulo*, 10/10/97; Lawrence Uzzell, "Aliança ortodoxo-comunista fere liberdade," in *O Estado de S. Paulo*, 10/6/97.

cow and all Russia. In Graz, it became obvious that the Orthodox were having difficulty accommodating to the *liberal* bent of the ecumenical groups. Once again came the *j'accuse* of the East against the aggressive proselytism of the other religious denominations .... Finally, a new Russian law on religious freedom, inspired by national religious protectionism, rekindled in the Catholic camp a nostalgia for Gorbatchev with his religious regulation of a more liberal bent."[118]

    * In a news release of March 9, 1998, Alexis II reaffirmed his conditions for the recovery of ecumenism: "It is necessary that both parts [the Catholic and the Russian Orthodox] condemn proselytism or the conversion of persons who belong to or are traditionally linked to the other confession."[119]

    * According to the Russian news service *Itar-Tass*, Archbishop Jean-Louis Tauran, after meeting with Alexis II (6/27/98), stated that conditions still did not exist for a meeting between the Pope and Russian patriarch.[120]

    In addition to the crisis in the ecumenical relations between the Catholic Church and the various Orthodox churches, which is evident from a simple reading of the events above, the fact cannot be ignored that within the schismatic milieu itself, division rules.

    First, one should note that among the churches in the Moscow patriarchate, one of the most important was the Ukrainian Orthodox church, headed by metropolitan Filarete of Kiev. However, due to a misunderstanding about the questions of hegemony and nationalism, this metropolitan was con-

---

[118] G. Valente, ibid.

[119] "Ortodossi - Alessio II: Difficile incontro con il Papa," in *30 Giorni*, March 1998, p. 53.

[120] Msgr. Tauran is considered as Vatican "minister of the exterior." "Tauran a Mosca: 'Migliora la situazione della Chiesa Cattolica,'" in *30 Giorni*, July-August 1998, p. 14.

demned by the Moscow synod. This opened a serious schism in the until then uniform Russian church.[121]

Second, on February 23, 1996, Russian patriarch Alexis II clearly demonstrated his rupture with patriarch of Constantinople Bartholomew I. In the official ceremony on the "Feast of the Angel," he did not cite Bartholomew I during the reading of the names of all the acting patriarchs.[122] The question of jurisdiction over the Orthodox church of Estonia gave rise to this impasse, which was called "undoubtedly the most serious crisis that the Orthodox church has undergone since the Schism between the Eastern and Western Church in 1054."[123]

The Russian Orthodox church, which claims half of the 200 million members worldwide, holds a place of irrefutable importance. Since the fall of the "Iron Curtain" and the dissolving of the USSR, it has been concerned about a certain number of national churches, the so-called independent or "self-governed" churches of its old republics and satellite countries, that have shown a propensity to become independent from the Moscow seat. Among these, some have chosen to place themselves under the "protection" of the patriarchate of Constantinople, which has been open to their requests. "Conflicts of jurisdiction have increased so much that in the last years it has become an explosive situation," one release reported candidly.[124]

Thus, Most Holy Father, already into the year 1999 that is preparing for the Millennium, the panorama of ecumenical relations with the schismatics is overcast with dark clouds. One

[121] Kirill de Smolensk, Interview granted to Giovanni Bensi, published under the title, "Mosca, alba di spine," in *Avvenire-Catholica,* 3/2/93.

[122] Laurent Grzybowski, "Orthodoxie - La déchirure," in *L'Actualité Religieuse,* 3/15/95, p. 10; "Igreja russa rompe com Constantinopla," in *Folha de S. Paulo,* 2/25/96.

[123] L. Grzybowski, "Moscou, Constantinople, à qui la première place?," in *L'Actualité Religieuse,* 4/15/96, p. 4.

[124] Ibid.

could say that the schismatics have been so long wary of ecumenism that an opening in this field is very improbable. If this conclusion, which follows indubitably from what has been presented above, is objective, why have You and the Holy See struggled unilaterally to continue an initiative that has been rejected by the other side?

Argumentandi gratia, let it be said that in every relationship there should be a reciprocity between the interested parties. Sadly, despite the fact that the schismatic party has shown clear signs of disinterest and even hostility, the Catholic side insists upon continuing negotiations, revealing a subservience that is hardly honorable. How could such an attitude be explained?

Doesn't it show that ecumenism is something artificial, which a certain progressivist current wants to impose, be it for or against Catholic doctrine and with or without the support of the other side? Doesn't such an ostensive manifestation of desire for union based on love begin to sound somewhat insincere? The facts at hand do not permit any further conjecture. For this reason, we come to You, Holy Father, to beseech You to clear the fog that has fallen over these matters and obscured a clear view.

2. Confusion and Decadence in the Protestant Groups

With regard to the Protestants, the situation of ecumenism presents no better a picture for its proponents. Since Protestantism is splintered into hundreds of smaller sects, it seems sufficient to present here only a few incidents in the relationship between the Catholic Church and two of its more important bodies: the World Council of Churches (WCC) and the so-called Anglican church.

A. The World Council of Churches: Phantom or Reality?

Obviously, Protestantism teems with division. Nothing could be more consistent, since Luther's principles call for revolt against authority, which generates disciplinary divisions. Free interpretation permits each one to understand the Scripture and, consequently, Faith and Morals, as he sees fit, which generates doctrinal divisions.

Founded in 1948 on the initiative of 147 Protestant and Orthodox sects, the largely protestant World Council of Churches (WCC) was conceived as a major force and voice of ecumenism. Nevertheless, from its very first meeting in Amsterdam, divisions were evident, certified by its first "Message" published on the occasion: "We are divided from one another not only in matters of faith, order, and tradition, but also by pride of nation, class, and race."[125]

In its central committee meeting in Toronto (1950), it became clear that the WCC represented participating sects neither in the realm of law nor the field of facts. A document that issued from that meeting admitted that the WCC was forged in a "debate of considerable intensity." It stated, "It is not a Super-church. It is not a world church. It is not the *una sancta* of which the creeds speak .... it cannot legislate or act for its member Churches." Further, it "has no specific doctrine about the nature of church unity."[126]

Therefore, the WCC reduced itself to a mere *forum* for debate: "The purpose of the World Council of Churches is not to negotiate unions between churches .... but to bring the churches into living contact with each other and to promote the

---

[125] Meeting in Amsterdam, "Rapport officiel," edited by W. A. Vissers't Hooft, Neuchâtel-Paris, apud Charles Boyer, verb. "Oecuménisme chrétien," in DTC, *Tables*, vol. III, col. 3349.

[126] C. Boyer, Ibid.

study and discussion of the issues of Christian unity."[127] Doing this, "it has no intention to impose any particular pattern of thought or life upon the churches."[128]

It is clear that the WCC lacks real substance and is not much more than a façade. Nevertheless, the mythology set in motion by progressivist propaganda strives to present it to Catholics as a powerful giant that unites in one single bloc a large number of Protestant sects as well as some of the Orthodox churches. Thus, the Catholic Church should treat this giant "representative" of the so-called Christian religions as an equal, dialogue with it, and satisfy its demands. Yet this sleight-of-hand propaganda hardly reflects the reality.

This picture was confirmed and updated by the report in *Le Figaro* of its 7th Assembly in 1991: "The 7th Ecumenical World Assembly of Churches, where more than 1,000 delegates and close to 3,500 participants met in Canberra [Australia], closed its sessions in a spirit of agitation. Women participants complained about sexual harassment in the housing arrangements at the university campus where the delegates were lodged. There was a violent scene involving the WCC general secretary, Uruguayan pastor Emilio Castro, and a young Canadian Anglican who was angry about the small number of youths at the assembly. Demonstrators even went so far as to carry placards accusing the Council of representing the Anti-Christ."[129]

Reports emphasized that the Russian Orthodox, Romanians, and Ukrainians were divided more by political matters than religious issues. Further, one of the most shocking elements of this Canberra Assembly was the free reign given to diverse spiritualities, particularly those of Asia. A large number of the

---

[127] Ibid.

[128] Ibid., col. 3353.

[129] Jean Bourdarias and Joëlle Dietrich, "Une odeur de soufre au VII Conseil Oecuménique des Églises," in *Le Figaro*, 2/26/91.

Western delegates were scandalized by ceremonies such as a pagan ritual presided over by a Korean woman delegate that ended with a crude aboriginal dance. "This mixture of elements from the Christian faith and of cultural elements that border on paganism," *Le Figaro* reported, "place the Christian message at risk, some of the participants objected. This was the principal accusation of the Orthodox delegates (who threatened to leave), who thought that by putting up with such debates the World Council had become nothing more than a crossroads for exchanging ideas."[130]

In a press statement in October of 1993, the new general secretary of the WCC, pastor Konrad Raiser, stated that the members were "far from the unitary optimism that existed even a short time ago. We see again that these profound divisions are not only the fruit of doctrinal and liturgical differences .... but of the diverse ways of the inculturation of Christianity in many places."[131]

In October of 1996, the WCC faced an even more profound crisis. Under the pretext of economic difficulties, some of the more important Protestant and Orthodox churches of the 330 member sects made a show of disapproval about the orientation of the entity and stopped contributing financially. They asked for a total reconstruction in the structure and objectives of the group.[132] Fr. René Beaupère, OP, an observer at WCC assemblies since 1968, confirmed the need for change, but said that he did not think the body would accept Raiser's proposals for reform. "I have some concerns," he said, "that his proposals have been delayed by this machine with its slow and sluggish gear-shifting and its great ignorance of the history of the ecu-

---

[130] Ibid.

[131] Benoît Vandeputte, "L'oecuménisme de transition de Konrad Raiser," in *La Croix*, 10/12/93.

[132] Geoffroy de Turckheim, "La crise de la cinquantaine," in *L'Actualité Religieuse*, 10/15/96, p. 12.

menical movement, the knowledge of which is indispensable for a full understanding of our present day problems."[133] He did not hide his disappointment in the plan for the group's new charter: "The document is truly defective, with no vision or inspiration. It is necessary to rewrite it completely. Curiously, the document is light-years behind the present day situation. I hope that the next version will be profoundly modified."[134]

Added to this general picture, extremely disappointing for the enthusiasts of ecumenism who had harbored such hope of success for the interconfessional initiatives, was a denouncement made of the group by Cardinal Joseph Ratzinger. At a book launching in Rome of a work on "liberation theology," Cardinal Ratzinger told journalists that "a large number of the Latin American Bishops have complained that the World Council of Churches had promoted and encouraged subversive movements that were prejudicial to the spreading of the Gospel."[135] Fr. Nicola Bux, author of *The Fifth Seal* published by Libreria Editrice Vaticana, noted that "during the '60s and '70s, there was a very strong third-world sentiment favoring Marxism in the West. Many Christian sectors, especially Protestant ones, supported Marxist movements and stimulated a movement inside Catholicism that affirmed 'liberation theology.'" Fr. Bux affirmed that the WCC had supported "the campaigns that helped the revolutions in Latin America."[136]

Thus, Most Holy Father, with regard to the WCC, it is not difficult to conclude that the group hardly represents the thinking of its participants. Because of the internal divisions that have affected its operation since its birth until today, it does

---

[133] René Beaupère, "Commentaries on the CEI," apud G. Turckheim, "Sous l'oeil d'un observateur catholique," Ibid.

[134] Ibid.

[135] Les accusations du Vatican," in *Le Figaro,* 6/10/97; "Protestantes financiam esquerda," in *Folha de S. Paulo,* 6/10/97.

[136] Ibid.

not offer the conditions needed to realize the dream of ecumenical unity. Far from promoting harmony and understanding, the group has supported subversive Marxist movements that work against the established order and stimulate internal turmoil in the Catholic Church. Therefore, in this case also, the ecumenical efforts realized since Vatican Council II reveal their fruitless, and even counter-productive, spirit. Once again, one could say this represents a failure of ecumenism. So we direct to Your Holiness a question: Why continue to pursue ecumenism with a group that does not present serious conditions of reciprocity?

B. The Anglican Church Reaches Its End

The perspective for the Anglican church is no less disheartening for proponents of ecumenism. A brief look at the internal structure and certain tendencies of the Church of England reveal serious factors of destabilization weighing over it.

First, the fact that it depends structurally on the English State makes it vulnerable. By an act of Parliament, it could suffer serious restrictions that could place its very existence at risk. It is no wonder that at times English Prelates have expressed fear: On one hand, they face a socialist parliamentary opposition to a church increasingly less frequented; on the other hand, they see a conservative opposition to a church that is more and more leftist in political, social, and economic matters.

Second, the clergy and hierarchy have taken on a growing moral permissivism, which looks lightly at moral transgressions and even serious sins that were banned in past times as inadmissible.

Third, the official decision of its Synod permitting the ordination of women (11/11/92) moved a step away from traditional Anglicanism and toward the more radical Protestant factions. This measure caused a serious internal problem since considerable numbers of the higher and lower clergy felt that they had been betrayed. This also stimulated thousands of members to leave the Anglican confession.

Fourth, all of these factors added fuel to the fire of those who hold that the Church of England has become decadent and is nearing its end.

To demonstrate these points, only a few reports will be presented. For example, illustrating the reaction to the increasing liberalism of customs in the Anglican clergy is the testimony of Ann Widdecombe, minister of Social Security in the government of Prime Minister John Major. On the day of her conversion to Catholicism when she received the Sacraments in Westminster Cathedral, she was asked about the internal situation in the Anglican church. She responded: "It seems the bishops are increasingly choosing adhesion to the world, instead of using their capacity to influence the world by their testimony of Faith. As far as what I have done, I am entering a Church that places the Faith before the style of the times, the Credo before compromise .... I am giving my adhesion to a Church that carries the Christian message to the world, and not the message of the world to Christians."[137] This testimony would seem to uphold a common view that the Anglican church has become a type of club among so many others to appease and appeal to a certain English mentality.

Professor Sheridan Gilley, head of the Department of Theology at the University of Durham, also converted to Catholicism. His explanation was even more profound: "England is losing its relationship with Christianity, and the Church of England has outlived its time as an institution. In order to understand what has happened, it is necessary to go back to the nineteenth century, when the rationalism of Hegel began to profoundly influence Christian thinking. The Catholic Church

---

[137] Ann Widdecombe, Statements to the press, apud Riccardo Cascioli, "Anglicani, quel ponti verso Roma," in *Avvenire*, 4/22/93.

combated Modernism; the Church of England, on the contrary, accepted it and added to this its pride of being a national church."[138] Prof. Gilley's astute observation associating Modernism with the decadence of the Anglican church is an insight that generally goes unnoticed.

Further on, he commented on today's moral laxity: "But the great change, above all in morals, took place in the '60s. Until then the Church of England was rigid, decidedly opposed to divorce and abortion, for example. In those years everything changed: The liberal wing predominated. The majority of bishops were intellectuals influenced by rationalism. Therefore, many of them today support the English law on abortion."[139]

This liberal trend in the sphere of morals is well-documented: "The Anglican church has given new proof of its capacity to adapt to the current times in a report about the family that it published yesterday. It said it supports a more positive approach to the situation of couples who live together without marriage. According to guidelines from the Committee for Social Responsibility presided over by Bishop Alan Morgan, the expression 'to live in sin' should no longer be used. This term represents a hardly positive attack upon a reality that is becoming increasingly common .... Furthermore, the report supports the position that the Church should receive homosexuals with open arms .... The text counsels Christians that they should not fall into the temptation of looking backward toward the 'golden age' of the family."[140]

Another commentator noted: "The Anglican church never ceases to amaze: It changes at such a speed that today it seems more like a social-democratic movement with ecological veins

---

[138] Sheridan Gilley, Interview granted to R. Cascioli published under the title, "Meglio convertito che liberal," in *Avvenire*, 5/6/93.

[139] Ibid.

[140] "La iglesia anglicana quiere la supresión del concepto 'vivir en pecado,'" in *El País*, Madrid, 6/7/95.

than a church based on Scripture. The *Times* reports: 'The bishops put adultery, abortion, euthanasia, and homosexuality on a
secondary plane. The priorities are Third World problems, un-
employment, social issues, and politics.' Two bishops clearly
stated that the church should be silent on the matter of adultery.
One added that it should not speak out on the subject of abortion. In short, the old morals have been overthrown.

"In the preface of the report [which gave the results of a
poll of 547 Anglican bishops] secretary general of the synod
Philip Mawer wrote that the poll showed 'how the Church of
England is in continuous evolution and is trying to find a better
way to carry out the will of Christ in the nation that it serves.'
Thus, even though homosexuality is a controversial subject,
none of the bishops believed that it was the most important
question, and 95% of them thought that it should be dealt with
openly. The case of gay priests, which many wanted to be freely
accepted in the Church, was raised in another place toward the
end of the synod by a letter signed by four primates."[141]

It is easy to see how serious the moral deterioration has
become in the Anglican milieu. Naturally speaking, one might
say that in face of today's moral laxity, a tragic outcome seems
unavoidable in the not too distant future.

A news report published in the London *Daily Telegraph*
and commented upon in the *Avvenire* (Rome) revealed the crisis
caused by the decision to ordain women. The commentator
noted: *"Have We Reached the End of the Church of England?
This Could be the Last Christmas before Anglicanism Is Reduced to Fragments.* This was the title of a long article published yesterday in the *Daily Telegraph,* a conservative newspaper in London that traditionally supports the monarchy and
State religion. The article noted that in the five years since the
decision of the Anglican synod to extend ordination to women,

---

[141] Alessio Altichieri, "Canterbury è rossa," in *Corriere della Sera,*
2/15/96.

some of the English hierarchy have developed the doctrine of "the tainted bishop," that is, bishops who defend the idea of women-priests but who cannot lay claim to the obedience of part of the clergy.

"The *Telegraph* reported that the statement of the Archbishop of Canterbury estimating that only 200 of the 10,000 Anglican pastors had resigned was considered a 'grotesquely optimistic' number by their own bishops. Further on, it noted that 'the majority of the Anglican clergy thought that it could not collaborate with bishops who granted orders to women. .... As a result, this might be the last Christmas that the clergy and the parishes of England celebrate together.'"[142] According to the report, one might expect that hundreds of Anglican priests could leave the Church of England.

In fact, it was not long before this prospect became fact. In February of 1993, information came to light that between one and three thousand Anglican pastors were moving toward conversion to the Catholic Church.[143] In April, the *Sunday Telegraph* reported the figure of one thousand.[144]

News analysts have described the precarious situation in which Anglicanism finds itself: "An earthquake opened in the Church of England when close to a thousand prelates (including some bishops) decided to take the 'big step.' For the motherhouse of Anglicanism this is a veritable schism. No more than about 10,000 priests serve .... the close to 28 million faithful in Wales and England. The repercussion of an exodus of such proportions upon 13,000 parishes, 50,000 schools, and numer-

---

[142] Antonio Perrini, "La chiesa inglese potrebbe spaccarsi entro un anno," in *Avvenire*, 12/19/92.

[143] A. Perrini, "Scisma a caro prezzo," in *Avvenire*, 2/20/93.

[144] "L'apertura dal Vaticano agli anglicani 'ribelli'?," in *Corriere della Sera*, 4/5/93; "Le Vatican prêt à accueillir des anglicans déçus," in *Le Figaro*, 4/5/93; Luigi Accattoli, "La Santa Sede apre agli anglicani pentiti," in *Corriere della Sera*, 4/7/93.

ous social organs of the Church of England could end by being massive."[145]

However, contrary to what one might expect, the representatives of the Catholic Church in England did not show any great zeal or haste to receive these wandering sheep who want to return to the flock of Christ. At the introductory meeting of the Catholic Primates to discuss this matter, Cardinal Basil Hume stated: "There is no doubt that we should not interrupt our ecumenical dialogue and amiable relations with the Church of England."[146]

At the end of the meeting, pastor Stephen Platten, assistant to Anglican archbishop George Carey, commented that he was "quite impressed by the ecumenical sensitivity that the Catholic English Bishops have shown in this situation. And I will truly be very surprised if they, either now or in the future, make decisions that offend the sensibility of our church."[147]

To speak more clearly, this seems to mean that the Catholic Bishops took the position of not supporting the conversion of the Anglicans. In fact, if there had been a real effort to receive those who beat upon the doors of the Catholic Church, certainly it would have meant the conversion of a considerable part of the British nation. Speaking to this point, a journalist noted, "If the Church of Rome had been more welcoming, one could suppose that the exodus of Anglicans would have been so great that identification between the State and the Anglican religion would no longer be justified. Add this to the crisis of the royal family, and one can understand why many of

---

[145] Salvatore Mazza, "Scacco alla Regina," in *Avvenire-Catholica*, 4/20/93.

[146] Basil Hume, Statements to the press, apud Riccardo Cascioli, "Chi bussa all'uscio di Westminster," in *Avvenire*, 4/21/93.

[147] Stephen Platten, Statements to the press, apud R. Cascioli, "È il giorno degli 'anglo-cattolici,'" in *Avvenire*, 4/23/93.

the English have the idea that an epoch is rapidly and ingloriously reaching its end."[148]

Thus, Most Holy Father, before the clear and tragic appeal of a thousand – and perhaps more – Anglican pastors and a large number of laymen who requested entrance into the Holy Church, the English Catholic Prelates, with their Cardinal at the head, opted for a "pastoral" way that would not destabilize the decadent and discredited Anglican church. More than simply a failure of ecumenical initiatives, a certain suspicion of complicity arises. Did not Our Lord Jesus Christ institute the College of Apostles, of which the Bishops are the successors, in order to evangelize the world and to convert men from false religions? How, then, could these English Catholic Prelates take such an attitude without violating this divine mandate?

Despite this conciliatory attitude on the part of the Catholic hierarchy toward the disintegrating Anglican Church, on the eve of the first ordination of women on March 13, 1994 in the cathedral of Bristol,[149] seven Anglican bishops and 700 pastors stated that they were converting to the Catholic Church, officially accepting the Primacy of Peter.[150] The document released to the public said that "only the Holy Roman Catholic Apostolic Church professes and teaches the revealed truth."[151]

In an interview, Anglican bishop Conrad Meyer explained his predicament that led to conversion: "For years I waited and prayed in silence. I suffered much within myself, but I held to the strong belief that one day the Anglican church

---

[148] R. Cascioli, "Chi bussa all'uscio di Westminster," in *Avvenire*, 4/21/93.

[149] "Anglicanos ordenam primeiras 32 mulheres," in *O Estado de S. Paulo*, 3/14/94.

[150] "Esodo degli anglicani - 'Torniamo dal Papa,'" in *Corriere della Sera*, 2/25/94.

[151] Riccardo Orizio, "Scisma in nome del Papa," in *Corriere della Sera*, 2/25/94.

would become Catholic, acknowledging once again the authority of the Pope and returning to the belief that the center of Christianity is Rome. When I and my friends realized that this reunification would not be possible, then we made our decision .... The Church of Rome is the only one who speaks out clearly on fundamental moral and doctrinal questions. It is this that that attracted us and it is for this that we feel the need."[152]

Most Holy Father, this question has certainly occurred to uncountable Catholics: What would have passed through the minds of bishop Meyer and his admirable companions in conversion when they learned that in the Encyclical *Ut unum sint* (n. 95), You placed that same Petrine Primacy that occasioned their enthusiasm and conversion at the mercy of the critiques and reforms of theologians – Catholic, Orthodox, and Protestant – in order to diminish it in its characteristics?

The picture of the crisis that has affected the so-called Anglican church could be summarized in the forceful words of well-known English journalist Paul Johnson. In his unique style, he notes: "I used to say that the Church of England, however bad it might be, was better than nothing. But I have changed my mind as I believe many other Catholics have done also. Anglicanism is too damaged: it has become so corrupt, its moral infirmity so apparent, and its infection so contagious that it has reached the point of constituting a risk of leprosy to other churches, including my own. I find it horrendous to read about these ecumenical conversations between Catholic and Anglican bishops. This is the road of spiritual death. I do not have any more doubts that the sooner the Anglican church as a national institution would shut down its activities, the better it would be for all – for its members, who have suffered for so long, for the Queen, for Parliament, for the country, and, not the least important, for Christianity .... Let us shed the old skin – or the re-

---

[152] Conrad Meyer, Interview granted to R. Orizio under the title, "Così ho capito che il Vaticano ha ragione. Il nostro futuro é Roma," Ibid.

mains of the Anglican decadence separated from the State – deprived of its old cathedrals and village churches, following its road to perdition, it is becoming nominally that which is taking place in reality: the Church of Sodom."[153]

One thing seems undeniable: a generalized and uncontrolled deterioration of the so-called Anglican church. In view of this picture, may Your Holiness permit us, as Catholics zealous for the exaltation of Holy Mother Church, to ask these questions: Since the Anglican church is falling apart, what is the real objective of ecumenism? Why does the Hierarchy continue to seek a unity of doctrine with persons who do not take this initiative seriously? And why are we helping to maintain the appearances of a hollow structure ready to collapse? From what has just been considered, one might say that if the Holy See would return to the wise and traditional practices of the apostolate prior to the Council, in a short time the just who long for reunion with Rome would convert and, with them, perhaps a large part of the English nation. Why, then, continue to strive for an unattainable and anesthetizing ecumenism?

3. Islam Advances – By Peaceful or Violent Means

The topic of inter-religious dialogue with the Muslims will be dealt with only *per summa capita*. In this overview, it easily could be proved that at the heart of the matter is the fact that the followers of Mohammed clearly show their intent to conquer Europe by a peaceful invasion.

First, this invasion is taking place by means of the gradual establishment of illegal immigrants in the West, a tactic that is receiving more and more support from the European Episcopates.

---

[153] Paul Johnson, "Anglicanismo, pecado original e a igreja de Sodoma," in *O Estado de S. Paulo*, 12/27/96.

Second, the work market has not complained because these immigrants afford a non-unionized and thus cheaper labor force in a Europe entangled in laws and labor processes.

Third, once established, the immigrants plan gradually to dominate the population by means of demographic expansion. At the same time, in countries characteristically European the birth rates are diminishing rapidly.

Fourth, immense investments of Arab money coming from the Persian Gulf oil regions are entering important sectors of the Western economy.

Fifth, mosques are proliferating with the friendly acquiescence of Catholic ecclesiastics, an undeniable sign of no strong desire to convert Muslims. It is impossible not to mention the construction of the largest mosque of Europe in Rome under the gaze and without the protest of Your Holiness. Further, this mosque was financed by the King of Saudi Arabia, a country that prohibits the construction of any Catholic Church.

Sixth, one could cite almost *ad infinitum* the number of cultural events and scholarships that favor Islam in Western universities, especially in Spain.

This "peaceful conquest" is but one of the arms in the Muslim tongs for dominion. The other is religious persecution of States or groups, which has also been increasing markedly. Religious persecution sanctioned by law occurs under the governments of Turkey, Saudi Arabia, Kuwait, Nigeria, Egypt, and Indonesia, as well as in Algeria, Sudan, Ethiopia, Burundi, Rwanda, Zaire, Yemen, Pakistan, and Afghanistan, countries in which so-called fundamentalist Islamic groups act with more or less freedom of movement. A principal characteristic of this persecution is the murder and oppression of Catholics – from Prelates to children. The number of assassinations, slaughters, and barbarous cruelties, including crucifixions and a new slave market, continues to grow.

Yet these are actions that are considered by many Muslims as an expression of a "holy war," the "anti-crusade" of

Islam. In fact, at a meeting in Khartoum (Sudan), the religious heads of 80 countries met together to relaunch a "holy war" with the aim of "emptying the Middle East of Christians."[154]

Placed before these facts, essential for anyone who would analyze the Muslim world and its relationship with the Catholic Church, how could one imagine sincerity on the part of the Muslims in what is called "inter-religious dialogues" with Islam? It seems clear, Most Holy Father, that the proposal to dialogue is taken by the followers of Mohammed as a sign of decadence in a Religion that seems to have abandoned the militancy of the Faith.

What is the use of the amiable messages that Cardinal Francis Arinze, president of the Pontifical Council for Interreligious Dialogue, sends every year to the Muslims on Ramadan in face of the aforementioned invasion and aggression that continues unabated? Inter-religious dialogue, whose aim would be to soften the *animus* of Islam, does nothing except to nourish its radicality.

Thus, Most Holy Father, it seems difficult not to see the failure of dialogue with the Muslims. With all respect we pose this question: Of what use is it to continue such dialogue? Further, for partisans of interconfessionalism, what would be the real purpose of a collective gathering of Catholics and Muslims at Sinai?

4. Characteristic Notes of the Judaic Establishment: Intransigence and Arrogance Toward the Church

Presenting the whole picture of Jewish relations is somewhat difficult: *First*, because the distinction between race and

---

[154] Barbara Stefanelli, "L'SOS dei cristiani arabi - Una contra-crociata ci minaccia: aiutateci a resistere," in *Corriere della Sera*, 5/11/95; Thierry Desjardins, "Les islamites en croisades," in *Le Figaro*, 3/31/95.

religion is not always clear, and *second*, because the Jews, like the Muslims, do not habitually distinguish between the spiritual and the temporal.

Taking principally the spiritual ambit as the reference point, it is evident that there are innumerable degrees of observance of the precepts of this confession. There is no single visible disciplinary authority to whom all must submit. In the opinion of the more religious Jews, there is a generalized acceptance of one same belief, of precepts that should be observed morally and liturgically, of certain laws that should govern the members that comprise the different social-political bodies – families, schools, groups, and the State of Israel. However, such common points do not form a single religious structure.

Perhaps the continuous nomadic lifestyle that characterized the people, perhaps because of the divergence of ideas and disputes of authority, there are a variety of religious rites, schools of thought, mystical exercises, juridical duties. This variance results from different interpretations of the various rabbinical schools of thought and their groups of followers. Therefore, one could say that in Judaism, as in the false Orthodox churches and Protestant sects, division reigns.

A contrario sensu, there is also a certain fluid, pneumatic unity that joins together Jews despite the variances. One of the principal factors that propitiates such a unity is opposition to the common enemy – the *goyim*, or that is, the non-Jew, according to certain precepts of the *Talmud*.[155] Since the inter-religious dialogue promoted by the Vatican acts as if it were dealing with a single body that is institutionally one, if we want to be coherent, we should seek unity in what is most characteristic in Judaism, that is, in the so-called orthodox Jews.

---

[155] Auguste Rohling, "Le juif selon le Talmud," apud Henri Delassus, *La conjuration antichrétienne*, Lille: Desclée de Brower, 1910, vol. II, pp. 691f.

The present Israeli government is supported by a political coalition in which the religious parties play a decisive role. With the growing influence of such parties, successive governments gradually have abandoned the policy of "pragmatism" that has characterized them since 1948[156] and have accentuated the theocratic note. "With a electoral growth of 50 percent in the last elections, the radical religious have become the most important part of Netanyahu's government," a recent report noted. "After resolving the complicated problem of putting together the new government, the radical religious are now beginning a new offensive to win even more influence in Israeli society. Controlling no less than six government ministries administering impressive funds, the religious ministers are attempting to impose their authority on politics .... giving it a strong religious cast capable of making palpable changes in society in the next four years. According to sociologist and anthropologist Nissan Bubin from the University of Barlan, the religious sector has achieved a shocking degree of influence due to the rapid growth of religiosity, mysticism, and the political coercion of the laity."[157]

The reaction in public opinion to the radical religious movement is also cause for concern. Ecclesiastical diplomats have a special capacity to assess this reality, which gives a certain credibility to the following report. A few years ago the Vatican Apostolic Nuncio in Israel, Archbishop Andrea di Montezemolo, said "that sentiments of intolerance against non-Jews are becoming more and more generalized in the Israeli population."[158]

---

[156] Abba Evan, "Israel volta ao pragmatismo dos fundadores," in *O Estado de S. Paulo*, 10/1/95.

[157] Guila Flint, "Escalada dos religiosos inquieta israelenses," in *O Estado de S. Paulo*, 9/1/96.

[158] "Há mais intolerantes em Israel, diz Núncio," in *Folha de S. Paulo*, 5/26/95.

Another factor that attests to the importance of the "or-thodox" is the influence that they have gained in the Israeli army, considered by many as the element that gives unity to the nation. In fact, the religious schools supply the volunteers who make up the elite of the Israeli army. The influence of the rabbis has reached such a point that some hold that the army would not obey a government order if it went against the religious interests of Israel, as, for example, a command to abandon the present-day territories.[159]

It is not surprising to find that in such a climate, laws against the Catholic Faith have been established. For example, an article in *Le Figaro* reported that a bill of law approved in the Knesset (parliament) "imposes a one-year prison sentence for the importation, printing, possession, reproduction, or distri-bution of religious documents that aim at conversion." Based on this, "Israel could make it illegal to possess a large number of Christian texts, beginning with the New Testament."[160] The measure broadens and extends an old prohibition that proscribes students from having a Bible with the New Testament, since this would "constitute an affront to the Hebraic faith of the stu-dents."[161]

Another example of intransigence and government sub-mission to the theocratic directives of the religious groups was Israel's clear violation of International Law when it declared Jerusalem its capital. The act that authorized the establishment of the State of Israel (1948) set up terms for the disputed Pales-tine territory (violated in the wars of 1967 and 1973) and estab-lished Jerusalem as a city that belonged to two peoples. Your

---

[159] Martine Gozlan, "Comment tu as change Israel!" in *L'Evenement de Jeudi*, 5/2-8/96.

[160] Philippe Gélie, "Le Knesset veut defendre le Nouveau Testament," in *Le Figaro*, 5/19/97.

[161] "Proibido o Novo Testamento nas escolas," in *30 Giorni*, February 1988, p. 47.

Holiness has not ceased to request a similar statute to safeguard the religious and historic character that the city has for the Catholic Church as well as for the Muslim and Jewish professions.[162] However, this has not been granted. In a press statement made on the vespers of his audience with the Pope, then-minister of the Exterior Shimon Peres categorically stated: "Jerusalem will never be an Arabic capital and the Hebrews will have no other capital except Jerusalem. Because Jerusalem is not just strategic, it is history."[163]

Certainly, if the ecumenical initiatives of Your Holiness were accepted, Jerusalem would look like a laboratory for ecumenical experiments, since it is the site where not only Catholics, Orthodox, and Protestants, but also Muslims and Jews would all reunite. However, this proposal, which would have given a strategic religious advantage to the proponents of panreligion, was rejected by the Jews. Therefore, the invitation for inter-religious understandings with the Jews also seems to be a closed matter.

Further, the attitude of Jewish authorities in their relations with the Catholic Church reveals a certain arrogance toward Catholic authorities. For example, there was the reprimand of chief rabbi of Rome Elio Toaff to Cardinal Camillo Ruini, then president of the Italian Episcopal Conference and Vicar of Rome. Cardinal Ruini had published meditations on the death of Our Lord, in which he stated that the leaders of the Hebrew people had decided to kill the Savior. This is an incontestable fact, narrated in various places in the New Testament. Yet rabbi Toaff arrogated to himself the right of rep-

---

[162] See Note 45 in Chapter I.

[163] Shimon Peres, Statements to the press, apud Maurizio Caprara, "Peres avverte il Papa: 'Gerusalemme non si divide, è la nostra capitale,'" in *Corriere della Sera*, 12/1/94.

rimanding the Cardinal, affirming that "this deals with a historic lie of which the Cardinal should be well aware."[164]

A second example: During the discussion about the gold that the Nazis took from the Jews and deposited in Switzerland, executive director of the Jewish World Council Elam Steinberg accused the Holy See of involvement in the robbery.[165] Yet it is a notorious fact that it was only through the magnanimity of Pius XII that the Jews of Rome were not deported to concentration camps. In fact, intimidated by the Nazi chief of police to pay 50 kilos of gold to avoid a mass deportation, the Jewish community of the Eternal City were only able to bring together 35 kilos. In desperation, the grand-rabbi of Rome, Israel Zolli, had recourse to Pius XII, who immediately gave 15 kilos to complete the package. The testimony comes from Rabbi Zolli himself, who later converted to Catholicism.[166]

Another attack on the role played by His Holiness Pius XII in the holocaust was made by chief rabbi of Israel Yisrael Meyer Lau. It was reported that "he [the rabbi] demanded a rigorous examination of the reasons that led to the silence of the Pontiff despite the dimension of the genocide."[167] In effect, rabbi Lau indirectly accused the Pope of complicity with the Nazi atrocities: "The lack of definition on the part of the Church at the rise of and during the holocaust and the uncov-

---

[164] Elio Toaff, Statements to the press, apud Bruno Bartoloni, "'Deicidio', è scontro," in *Corriere della Sera*, 4/24/92.

[165] "Vaticano é pressionado a abrir seus arquivos," in *Jornal do Brasil*, 12/5/97.

[166] Tommaso Ricci, "Conversão, ou melhor, chegada," in *30 Dias*, March 1991, p. 69.

[167] Yisrael Meyer Lau, Statements to the press, apud Henry Raymont, "Judeus querem reexame de relatório sobre holocausto," in *O Estado de S. Paulo*, 4/14/98.

ering of the role of the one who led the Church, Pius XII, is still not acceptable to us."[168]

Perhaps the most significant episode of Jewish repudiation of inter-religious dialogue is what took place in Israel when the Archbishop of Paris, Cardinal Jean-Marie Lustiger, was invited to address an international conference at the University of Tel Aviv. The conference, whose theme was *The Silence of God During the Holocaust,* made up part of a series of commemorations celebrating Holocaust Memorial Day. Cardinal Lustiger is himself of the Jewish race and claims that his conversion to the Catholic faith did not mean that he had abandoned Judaism, but signified the harmonic summation of the two faiths.[169]

The news of his invitation to the University of Tel Aviv aroused strong reactions in religious circles of Israel. When chief rabbi Meyer Lau learned of this, he spoke out forcefully: "I would have nothing against the participation in the conference of someone who was not a Jew, who had never betrayed his people, his nation, and his faith." Continuing, the rabbi predicted the return of Lustiger to Judaism in terms that reveal his anti-ecumenical position: "Perhaps he will feel repentance and sorrow, and return to Judaism .... I am not speaking of the person. I am speaking of the concept of baptism: it is a danger to the Jewish existence."[170] A press report commented on this reaction: "On September 21, 1993, grand rabbi Lau was received by John Paul II. Today he marked his boundaries to

---

[168] Y. M. Lau, Statements to the press, apud *Folha de S. Paulo,* "Para judeus texto é ameno demais," 3/17/98.

[169] Jean-Marie Lustiger, Interview granted to Israeli TV, apud Reali Junior, "Israel veta Cardeal de Paris," in *Jornal da Tarde,* São Paulo, 4/26/95.

[170] Y. M. Lau, Statements to the press, apud Pierre Rousselin, "La conversion critiquée di Cardinal Lustiger," in *Le Figaro,* 4/24/95.

religious dialogue between Jews and Christians. He called Cardinal Lustiger a traitor."[171]

When the Cardinal arrived in Israel, rabbi Meyer repeated his accusations: "By Abraham Lustiger becoming Jean-Marie Lustiger, he betrayed his people and his religion. He incarnates the way of spiritual extinction that leads, like the physical destruction, to the 'final solution' for the Jewish problem."[172] Another commentator, who considers rabbi Lau a moderate and a "great supporter of dialogue with the Church," attributed even stronger statements to Lau: "Lustiger is an apostate who abandoned our people at the most dramatic moment." To this, the reported commented: "The ice appears once and for all – as in the worst periods of conflict between the two religions."[173]

The president of the International Council of Yad Washem (holocaust museum), Dr. Yossef Burg, was reported to say that "someone who has converted to Christianity no longer belongs to the Jewish people and should not participate in an official ceremony."[174] The newspaper, trying to show a certain impartiality, noted that "despite the disgust caused in many of us by a Jewish apostate who converted to Catholicism during the holocaust, we are not asking him to preach, but only to speak at an academic conference." It added that in itself this did not signify an "implicit acceptance" of his conversion.[175]

---

[171] Élie Marechal, "Le choix fervent de Mgr. Lustiger," in *Le Figaro*, 4/25/95.

[172] Y. M. Lau, Statements to the press, apud P. Rousselin, "Ce Cardinal qui serait de trop en Terre Sainte," in *Le Figaro*, 4/25/95.

[173] Lorenzo Cremonesi, "L'olocausto divide ebrei e Vaticano," in *Corriere della Sera*, 4/27/95.

[174] P. Rousselin, "La conversion critiquée," Ibid.

[175] Ibid.

Rabbi David Rosen, Director of Interfaith Relations and co-liaison to the Vatican, said that he believed that the participation of Lustiger in the Israeli Holocaust Memorial Day conference was "a grave error." Questioned by the press, he stated that "conversion for the Jews is not a theological question, but an act of betrayal. Our society is still incapable of facing the question."[176] Rosen tried to explain that "in this country there is still a very deep distrust regarding everything that is linked to the Church. And Lustiger incarnates the most widespread stereotype, one in Christianity who tries to convert Jews."[177]

These reports, Most Holy Father, seem to leave no doubt that these Jewish leaders and their followers, so far as they represent the religious establishment, do not desire the inter-religious dialogue proposed by the Vatican. They have "a very deep distrust" of the Catholic Church.

A question naturally arises from these considerations: Where is this dialogue heading, since the Jewish partner does not want to adapt to anything other than its own precepts? Should there be, perchance, a continual modification of the Church, the sources of Revelation, her dogmas and history, in order not to offend the followers of the Jewish creed? Is this what could be intended by a common declaration of "faith" to be made at a meeting at the top of Mount Sinai?

How can one not think that this would be the only position acceptable to the Jews, but absolutely unacceptable to Catholics? Therefore, Most Holy Father, one could say that either the Catholic Church renounces her own characteristics or religious dialogue with Judaism is impossible. Would not this position be a failure for the proponents of interconfessional union?

---

[176] David Rosen, Statements to the press, Ibid.

[177] L. Cremonesi, Ibid.

Having analyzed ecumenism in relation to the Orthodox and Protestants, as well as in its attempts to dialogue with the Muslims and Jews, it is clear that the interconfessional initiatives of the Vatican present no possibilities of success with any of these false religions. Therefore, Most Holy Father John Paul II, everything indicates that the plans for the Millennium festivities are being projected by persons who are not taking into account the actual reality. Far from tending toward a panreligion, Islam and Judaism show a notable increase of ardent and radical followers moved by an imperialist ideology. Should things continue along the same pathway, what is being prepared is a future quite different from the one dreamed of by those inspired by pacifist longings for dialogue...

*   *   *

CONCLUSION

Upon closing this letter, Most Holy Father, we beg leave to present some final considerations by way of conclusion.

On the occasion of Vatican Council II, the men who were directing the destiny of the Church committed a grave error. They judged that the bourgeois world would last forever. They sought to satisfy modern man's material desires and to nourish the illusions of an euphoric post-war world. The conciliar policy of *aggiornamento* was planned to accommodate such aspirations. Yet the Council was hardly over and a dark storm began to appear on the horizon. Its dense clouds were formed by a growing nausea and ennui for that bourgeois world that was becoming so oppressive with its unrelenting pursuit for pleasure, power, and money. In May of 1968 the students of the Sorbonne unleashed a protest that marked the beginning of the end of the ideal models of the modern world and became a paradigm of the new stage of the Revolution. An analysis of the consequences of this anarchic revolt and of the evil that it represented – since it attacked indiscriminately the mediocrity of the bourgeoisie along with the perennial values that had sustained society until then – can be found in *Revolution and Counter-Revolution*, the masterful work of Prof. Plinio Corrêa de Oliveira.[178]

The Conciliar Church, celebrating its nuptials with the modern world, especially in the Constitution *Gaudium et spes*, did not perceive that it has espoused a dying man. And the optimism of the times that accompanied this ephemeral "hon-

---

[178] Plinio Corrêa de Oliveira, *Revolution and Counter-Revolution,* York, PA: The American Society for the Defense of Tradition, Family and Property, 1993, part. III, chap. III, pp. 156-166.

eymoon" of the Church and the modern world would soon be transformed into apprehension and anguish.

A lamentable error, the adaptation of the Church to the world! Long will it be remembered by those who dedicate themselves to the analysis of historical panoramas. All the more so in that it is very rare to see the Vatican err, even in the social-psychological ambit. In fact, the Vatican's proverbial political wisdom, its incomparable diplomatic style, its profound understanding of situations, place it on a plateau far above any other institution. However, despite this, the reality is undeniable: At the Council, the men who directed the Vatican erred.

Throughout the document that closes here, Most Holy Father, attempts have been made to show how ecumenism, inter-religious dialogue, and the festivities prepared for the Millennium do not appear to be in conformance with Catholic Doctrine (Chapters I and II); further, even for the parties involved, these ecumenical initiatives are, with a frequency worthy of attention, considered to have deteriorated (Chapter III). From this analysis a clear picture emerges. Ecumenism and inter-religious dialogue are passing through a grave crisis, which could put at risk their very existence.

Nonetheless, it was precisely at this moment as we approach the year 2000 that the advisers of the Pope have chosen to make a grand ecumenical effort on the occasion of the passing of the Millennium. From this two questions inevitably arise: Were these advisers unaware of this crisis, and because of this, did they optimistically launch this initiative? Or were they cognizant of the reality and nevertheless still trying to force the situation and turn back this failure of ecumenism? It would be desirable to have clear answers for these questions.

Whatever be the case, one can ask: Are we now heading toward committing an error similar to the one verified above regarding Conciliar relations with the modern world? The present error would be twofold: *First*, to close one's eyes to how this ecumenism conflicts with Catholic Doctrine; *Second*, to ignore the parties to the dialogue who are not disposed to accompany the next steps desired by the Holy See.

If this analysis is objective, where would this error lead us? The politics of "no return" in relation to ecumenism and to inter-religious dialogue would seem to run the risk of crystallizing large sectors of Catholic opinion, perhaps threatening the unity of the Church itself. This concern is even more worthy of your attention since the Millennium festivities seem to be conceived in a way that stimulates the initiatives of the more radical wings of Catholic progressivism.

Could it not be possible that the reaction of counter-revolutionary Catholics and the advance of the progressivists could collide and steer out of control? Where would this lead the Church except to a situation of profound convulsion?

If, however, the direction that the Church is taking was not prompted by the initiative of your advisers, but Your Holiness is also aware of the panorama and the dangers that have been exposed here, permit us then, as a final plea, with all respect and moved by the most profound concern, to ask You: *Quo vadis, Petre?*

The humble and obedient servant of the Papacy in Our Lord Jesus Christ and the Blessed Virgin Mary,

Atila Sinke Guimarães

*

FINAL PRAYER

Given the seriousness of the matter, it seems proper at this moment to look beyond all earthly powers toward Heaven itself: to Our Lady of Sorrows, the Queen of Carmel, the Virgin of Fatima, who in 1917 – under these three invocations – delivered a message by way of three peasant children to Catholics and to the world. To Her, then, the author presents these final questions and requests.

Our Lady of Sorrows, who did participate by the merits of your Co-Redemption in the Divine omniscience, did you not know, already in 1917, the sufferings to which Holy Mother Church would be subject in this year of 1999? Why, O Lady, did you not leave a warning, a sign, that might allow your faithful children to discern the evil that was infiltrating the Church and that is transforming it into an institution different from what it was? Or would the part of the secret of Fatima that has not yet been revealed deal precisely with this point? In that case, who has been responsible for withholding this secret? Why have Catholics been prevented from knowing the contents of this message of alert? Thus we implore you, Our Lady of Sorrows, to save the Catholic Church from sufferings even greater than those of our days.

Queen of Carmel, come to the aid of your Church! You were venerated since the early days of History by the Prophet Elias when, at the top of Mount Carmel, he implored an end to the drought that lay waste the land. Then you were symbolized by a small cloud that gradually grew larger and brought rain, fertility, and abundance. Come now, O Queen of Carmel, and end the terrible drought that chastises Holy Mother Church! Make the reign of the Kingdom of Your Immaculate Heart that you promised at Fatima fall upon the earth: *"In the end my Im-maculate Heart will triumph!"*

Virgin of Fatima, who asked the Pope to make a solemn consecration of Russia to The Immaculate Heart of Mary in union with all the bishops of the world as a condition to bring about the conversion of that country and to avoid a universal chastisement, we ask you: Has the moral and cultural crisis of the world intensified because the requests of the Blessed Mother were not followed? Would the consecration that was made not have fulfilled the demands you made and, therefore, be invalid? Nothing indicates that this consecration has been received by Thee as an offering with "an odor of sweetness in the sight of the most High" (Eccles. 35:8) so that you would with-hold the announced chastisement.

Finally, over and beyond these questions about the con-secration, how can it not be asked: Is not the Church now living through a most terrible chastisement? For when has History wit-nessed in the Church a greater institutional dissolution, so great a doctrinal confusion and moral laxity, so profound a hermeneutic relativism and loss of liturgical solemnity, such intense exegetical antagonism with the past, and such immense canonical liberal-ism? We beg you, Our Lady of Fatima, through your interces-sion, shorten this period of chastisement. Close, in this last year of the Millennium, this period of evil and deign by your guidance and enlightenment to usher in a new era in which the Holy Catholic Church and your name, O Lady, shall be glorified as never before!

*   *   *

In The Murky Waters of Vatican II
by Atila Sinke Guimarães

◆ First Volume of the powerful 11-volume Collection *Eli, Eli, lamma sabacthani?* (My God, My God, why hast Thou abandoned me?

◆ The result of over 15 years of study and research. An objective study of the letter, spirit and thinking of the documents of Vatican II.

"This book is MAGNIFICENT! It is going to be THE reference book of Vatican II well into the 21st century."   - Fr. Malachi Martin

"Obviously I admire this book - both for the strength of its scholarship and its conclusions, which are the best explanation I have yet seen of what the Council did. ... In fact, I suggest you buy three copies: one for yourself, one for a seminarian, pastor or religious, and one for your bishop."   - Rev. Charles Fiore

"Every Catholic concerned about the crisis in the Church should secure a copy of this book for their library and become familiar with its content. It promises to serve as an invaluable reference tool for years to come." - John Vennari, *Catholic Family News*

"A bold and timely contribution to the Church's contemporary self-reflection."   - Fr. Brian Harrison, O.S., Ph.D., St.D., *Pontifical Catholic University of Puerto Rico*

"I hope and pray that you will continue publishing the succeeding volumes of this remarkable, valuable work - and SOON! With my priestly blessing,   - Rev. Robert A. Skeris, Ph.D., *Christendom College*

*"The **Appendix on Homosexuality** is worth the price of the book all in itself."*   - Mrs. Solange Hertz, *The Remnant*

AVAILABLE WORKS BY ATILA SINKE GUIMARÃES

❖ *In the Murky Waters of Vatican II* $15 each
❖ *Quo Vadis, Petre?* $8 each 2/$15 (Quantity discounts available)
❖ *We Are Church: Radical Aims, Dangerous Errors* $5 each 3/$12
❖ *Toward the Year 2000: Archbishop Quinn's Strange Council* $3 each - 3/$7.50

(Add $3.00 shipping for each order)

TRADITION IN ACTION, INC.
PO BOX 23135 - LOS ANGELES, CA. 90023